A Pawn of Fate

A true story of a search for identity

RITA KEELEY BROWN

Outskirts Press, Inc.
Denver, Colorado

Contents

Part One

Chapter One

Climbing the path toward her home after a long day in the rice fields, Liu Qiu Ying was moving slower than usual. Sharp pains in her abdomen told her contractions were starting. Her hour to deliver the baby was near. She prayed that she would be in her home and not out in the fields when the baby insisted on coming. The path wound along the side of a mountain for about half a mile. It meandered through pine trees, banana trees, and bamboo that rose up through a carpet of vines, ferns, and prairie grass. As a strong contraction began she grabbed a pine branch for support and grimaced as her abdomen hardened and the pain followed. When the pain subsided and her muscles relaxed, she opened her eyes. She realized she was standing opposite the hillside that held the graves of two of her other children who had died of starvation. Might that, too, become the fate of this child about to be born?

Staying alive was extremely difficult not only for Ying, her husband, Chin Yin Zhong, and their 11-year old son, Chin Yuen Xu, but for everyone in their small village and

1

throughout the whole of China in 1939. It was a time of turmoil and danger from many sides. Not only had Japan declared war and invaded China, there was a rapidly growing internal threat of a Communist takeover of the established Chinese government. There were warring factions within the country as well as from the outside.

Ying could hear Japanese bombers rumbling high overhead in the distance as she made her way along the path. This was a terrifying sound to her bringing a shiver of fear as she scanned the sky to make sure they were not headed in her direction. Thousands had been killed in bombings and ground attacks and thousands more were dying of starvation. Villages and cities were being invaded, plundered, and burned to the ground. Her village was Wen Qian Yu Hui, a small remote village in the mountains about 200 miles southwest of Canton in the Guangdong Province. It was off the beaten track from the larger cities where most of the attacks took place, but everyone knew that this could change at any moment. What loomed strong in the minds of all villagers was the fact that their life and the lives of everyone in the 50 families who lived there could be quickly snuffed out.

Though this remote location brought tentative security from direct attack, it created another kind of hardship. Being so isolated cut them off from the rapidly dwindling outside sources of food, clothing and other necessities and blocked the one resource for marketing their products. The nearest city, Toi Shan, was at least fifteen miles away. There was no transportation except for a few bicycles. Everyone walked wherever they needed to go. Ying's family had to live on whatever they could provide for themselves. They were totally dependent on what they could grow and the animals they could raise. When their supplies were gone there were no replacements available. Supplies had to last until the next growing season with the hope that the animals would also survive and reproduce in sufficient numbers.

The government allotted each family three acres to farm. Unfortunately, much of the land in China is not arable. Whatever land you were given, good or bad, you had to work with as best you could. Oftentimes the soil was very rocky and difficult to cultivate. The fields were about half a mile from the village and accessible only on foot. Any tools needed or food harvested must be carried to and from the fields. If the village was lucky there might be a water buffalo available to do the plowing.

The main crops were rice, peanuts and vegetables. They also raised chickens, ducks, geese and pigs. A nearby pond provided a limited supply of fish that they could catch and eat. The frogs, mice and snakes in and around the fields provided many a meal. When their food supply was depleted, they were forced to eat their rice and bamboo seedlings. This meant that future crops would become more and more sparse. At times their situation became so desperate and the people so hungry they fought with each other over the slop to be fed to the pigs. "How will we feed yet another?" Ying wondered in her heart.

Houses in the village were built close together along each side of a narrow alleyway. The walls of the houses were made of mud formed from a mixture of clay, reeds, and animal dung. There were no doors that could be closed, only an open entryway and a few windows. Everything was wide open. They used animal skins sewn together to block the openings during inclement weather. Each house consisted of a kitchen, living room, bedroom, and a loft totaling about 200 square feet. All the floors were dirt except for the living room area that had a concrete floor. That was where the family gathered to eat their meals. The roof was constructed of a wood lath base covered with thin red tiles. Fortunately, this is an area of mild climate where the weather never turns very cold except at the highest elevations.

In the 1930s there was no electricity and their only water source was a public well. Water had to be carried in buckets hung on long bamboo poles across their shoulders from the well to their homes or to the fields to water their crops.

Cooking was done in pots/woks set low in a hearth on top of firewood lit from underneath or hung on a tripod frame above the flames. Water for laundry or bathing was also heated in this way.

The pigsty was located outside the kitchen and living room area. Although it was kept very clean, it was still the area where an average of ten pigs lived. The chickens, ducks and geese were kept behind the back of the house. As the breeze shifted so would the pervading odors. The smell of the animals could be overpowered by the delicious smell of the rice, meat, and vegetables cooking in the kitchen, or the reverse, when the wind changed and animal smells would dominate.

With no doors on the houses, the chickens and ducks could wander in and out. It would not be unusual to awaken with a chicken or duck asleep at your feet or even on your head. Animals were part of the family.

When an animal had to be slaughtered for food no part was wasted. Not only did the animal provide the main part of their dinner, this dinner was stir-fried in lard from the pig, goose or whatever animal was slaughtered. Their pillows and mattresses were stuffed with the feathers of the ducks, geese and chickens. Skins and bones had numerous uses from clothing to tools. They could not afford to waste a thing and found a use for every part of the animal.

A Pawn of Fate

Her husband, Zhong and their son, Xu, were watching for her when she reached the end of the path. They were aware that she was moving slower these days and knew that soon there would be a fourth member in their family.

Chapter Two

Young Chester Lee was both excited and a little scared. It was September and school would be starting soon. His mother was going to take him shopping to get new clothes, school supplies and a lunch box. They would be riding the streetcar to shop at those huge stores downtown. This was all very new and a bit overwhelming to him. Starting school is a big time in any boy's life, but especially daunting for him, being Chinese when it seemed everyone else was not. He did look forward to being with children his own age and meeting new friends.

Chester lived with his parents in the third largest city in the United States, right in the heartland of America – Chicago, Illinois. Chicago is a city of over two million people and offered every imaginable sight, sound and venture to hold a bright young boy's interest. There was so much to learn about and to understand.

His parents, Victoria and Harry Chin, owned a restaurant called *The Paris Inn*. The restaurant specialized in serving Cantonese food, but also served excellent American food. It was originally owned by a relative of Victoria's who hired Harry as a busboy and that was how the two met, and later, married.

Harry was born in China in 1910. When he came to America in his teens he had only the equivalent of a third-grade education. When he arrived in Chicago he applied for work at the restaurant and, when hired, worked 16-hour days. He lived in the restaurant's food storage area where the potatoes and onions were kept. It was a small room with a dim overhead light. After work he would sit with a Chinese-English dictionary and the Chicago Tribune. With these two resources he taught himself to read and write English. Growing up in China he had learned to be very vigilant of any resources that came his way. He was very careful with his money and saved almost every penny he earned. He always paid for everything in cash. This habit prevailed throughout his life and came to include items like cars and houses. Years later, after they had married, Victoria's relative who owned the restaurant decided to move away, and sold the restaurant to Victoria and Harry. Harry had saved enough cash to buy it, and because it was important to Victoria's relatives to keep the restaurant in the family, this worked out well for everyone.

Victoria was eight years older than Harry. Her birth records state that she was born in California in 1902. Her family later moved to Chicago to join their relatives. While Harry was a very quiet and unassuming type. Victoria, on the other hand, was someone who almost everyone feared. She was rigid in her outlook on life and in her demeanor. She was authoritarian and had a razor-sharp tongue. If you caused her the slightest difficulty you would hear about it in no uncertain terms and at length. She was not one you would go to for warm fuzzies.

Chester was their only child and lived under her constant scrutiny. As parents, they provided him with all the material things needed to do well in life and saw to it that he had a good education. Victoria and Harry gave Chester everything he could need except the one thing a child needs most - a warm, loving relationship.

When he began elementary school, his teacher told Victoria that they must speak to him in English at home. He was a good student and quickly became proficient in English. He then, did not want to speak Chinese at all. His friends spoke English and he saw no need for fluency in Chinese. This did not please his parents. Chester still understood Chinese and would converse in it as required by his parents. They wanted him to be Chinese first, American second. His mother enrolled him in an after-school all-Chinese program for learning to read and write the language. After a long day at school Victoria would take him on an hour-long streetcar ride to Chinatown for the lessons. This added a total of three hours of involvement in more schooling about something he didn't want to learn anyway. Her efforts were futile as he simply had no interest in knowing or speaking Chinese and after a few years, the Chinese schooling stopped.

He knew enough basic Chinese to handle himself in situations that might arise at the family restaurant where he helped out after school and on weekends or when getting together with relatives. That was as far as he wanted go with it. He saw no real need for all this Chinese stuff. After all, his father had named him Chester after the 21st President of the United States of America, Chester Arthur. Chester saw himself as an American who happened to look Chinese and this sometimes got him into trouble with other kids. Prejudice against Asians was strong and was heightened after Pearl Harbor. To this day he bears a scar on his forehead from rocks thrown at him in elementary school.

Baseball was big in Chicago and Chester loved the

game. This was one thing he learned from and shared with Harry. The Chicago Cubs and the Chicago White Sox, along with the Brooklyn Dodgers, were his favorite teams. His heroes were Ernie Banks and Hank Sauer from the Cubbies, Nelson Fox and Jim Rivera of the Sox. He was already hoping that for his next birthday, on May 14th, he could to go to a White Sox or Cubs game.

Chicago was a beautiful, bustling city at the hub of commerce, transportation, and finance and was growing rapidly. It was noted for its universities, libraries, fine arts and beautiful buildings as well as for its huge stockyards and meat-packing industry. There was water, water everywhere. Located at the lower tip of Lake Michigan, the second largest of the five Great Lakes, it also had the Chicago River running through its downtown center. This river had historical importance because it provided the final link to the Mississippi River from New York. This made possible a waterway from Albany, New York through the Erie Canal and the Great Lakes to the Mississippi all the way down to New Orleans, Louisiana. This was a pivotal point in the westward expansion of the country. It opened the door to the West and gave stability to the new United States of the 1800's. It stirred the pioneer spirit of the people. What an important and historical city to be living in. As a young boy just starting school Chester could not be aware of or absorb much of this, but as he grew older and learned more about his city he would realize why it was such a magical place to live.

By this time in the 1940s, almost every family in the neighborhood had their own radios, refrigerators, washing machines and many of the other rapidly developing technical advancements in easy living. Many also had cars and even television.

Cars were a luxury more than a necessity because the

city had developed a wonderful system of surface and elevated trains that could get you almost anywhere you needed to go in the city and surrounding towns for the amazing sum of ten cents. Chicago became one of the most important transportation centers in the country - the hub for airlines and trains. Large ships and barges sailed into and out of the port of Chicago carrying all kinds of commercial products.

People living here had access to almost anything they could possibly want. Their only complaint might be the weather. Chicago is known as "The Windy City" and for good reason. Strong winds (an average of 30-50 miles per hour) blow off the lake and swirl through the town. This is a year-round phenomenon. In the winter, when temperatures go way below freezing and the edges of the lake actually freeze, those winds bring an intense cold that no amount of warm clothing can stop. Today underground passageways have been built connecting many of the large downtown buildings so people don't have to go outside in such freezing cold and wind.

This was Chester Lee's world in which to grow up and become whatever he wanted to be.

Chapter Three

It was not long before a new voice joined the chorus of chickens clucking, ducks quacking, geese honking, and pigs grunting. The new voice was the cry of a newborn baby boy. Chin Yuen Yick was born in the little loft at the back of the house. The day of his birth was May 28, 1939. It was only a day or so later that he was out in the rice fields sleeping in a sling tied around his mother's back. A mother in this village had not the luxury of even a few hours, let alone days, for recovery and adjustment to a new baby in the household. It was – have the baby, clean up after yourself, and get back to work. There were no doctors or midwives in attendance. The most a woman could hope for would be some small assistance from family and neighbors if they could be spared from work in the fields.

This new baby was Liu Qiu Ying's fourth child. She was 31 years of age and her husband, Chin Yin Zhong, was 40. They were both in relatively good health although Zhong was quite crippled from an attack of smallpox in his youth. The infection had caused his hands and legs to be severely disabled. He was not able to make the trek to work in the fields and had to remain doing what work he could in their home and around the village. He was a proud man. Even though he was starving, he would never accept an offer to eat at the house of someone who hired him to work.

Ying provided the main support of the family. Besides working in the fields she was an excellent seamstress and earned money sewing dresses for others. She was able to recreate a dress just by studying the style. She could then reproduce it in whatever fabric the person had selected. She was a very intelligent, strong and determined woman.

Two of their children had died of starvation when there was simply not enough food to give them the nourishment they needed for a strong start in life and resistance to illness. The two children that died were both girls.

The oldest boy, Chin Yuen Xu, now eleven years old, was a strong boy who was able to survive and be of help to his parents. He was excited about having a brother. Girls were not prized as much as boys in the Chinese culture. It has long been a Chinese tradition that when a girl grows up and marries she becomes part of her husband's family and no longer contributes to her family. A boy, when he grows up and marries, adds to their family work force with a wife and children. It also becomes the grown son's responsibility to care for his aging parents. Female children did not enhance the family situation and thus were regarded as more of a burden overall.

Great turmoil reigned within China besides the Japanese invasion that had become an all-out war in 1937. The Chinese Nationalists under Chiang Kai Shek, or as he is now called, Jiang Jieshi, were in power but their control was rapidly weakening. They were fighting the Japanese as well as trying to stem the rise of Communism. Equipment and manpower were stretched to the limit. The Communist Revolution continued to gain strength and took over the country entirely and officially in 1949. The remaining Nationalist government and its supporters fled and relocated in Taiwan.

As the Communist government took over mainland China they issued decrees regarding life under the new regime. One such decree was that families living in the city were to have only one child. Families living in the farming villages needed more hands to be able to work in the fields, so for them this policy was not as strongly enforced, but they were supposed to have no more than two children.

As a result of the low regard for female children, atrocities were known to occur. Some of these were government-induced and others were considered to be matters of basic family survival. Cause of death could be described as "accidental choking", "born dead" or such. Doctors were encouraged to "make sure a baby girl does not live" and/or give lethal injections. Females simply had little value in the long-range family situation. Each morsel of food had to be shared and those morsels were very scarce. The fewer people to share it with, the better the chance of survival for the more critical family members.

This same instruction to doctors applied to children born deformed or mentally retarded. At this time neither the government nor the family had a way to provide for the special care and needs of these children. It is almost impossible for anyone in the western world to even imagine such a situation, but there, in that desperate situation, it became a matter of the survival of the fittest. Females and the disabled had little chance. If the only child was female, her value increased slightly as she was, at least, another pair of hands to do chores necessary for the existence of the family.

Now Ying and Zhong had another mouth to feed. How would they manage it? Could this child survive and be healthy? Could they survive another child's death from starvation? These thoughts were a constant heavy weight on Ying's heart and mind as she nursed this new life. He did seem a strong hearty little one, but his chances of survival were slim.

As little Yick grew it became clear that he was a very active, strong-willed child. He quickly learned to run for cover when the Japanese airplanes flew over and to stay hidden until the planes could be heard no longer. He was well known for having a very mischievous streak. He loved playing pranks on his best friend, Zhi Ling. He especially loved to take advantage of him at inopportune moments. When his friend would squat with his pants down around his ankles to do his potty business that was Yick's favorite time to give him an impish shove and run off as fast as he could.

When he was about three or four years old an older woman in the village wanted to adopt him. After thinking about it for a long time and talking it over with Zhong, Ying decided that maybe it would be best for him if they did allow him to be adopted. The woman lived nearby, so they would be able to see him and know how he was doing. This woman should be able to do much more for him than they ever could. With a heavy heart she took him to the woman and agreed to the adoption.

For weeks she couldn't face seeing him with someone else. Finally she could stand it no longer and went to the street where the woman lived to see how her son was doing. She was horrified at what she saw! He was dressed in dirty ragged clothes and was so dirty himself that he could hardly be recognized. He was playing in a filthy debris-strewn yard. It was an awful situation. She entered the yard, took her child back and told the woman their deal was off and returned whatever the woman had given her for the adoption. She could not stand seeing him like that. They would work it out somehow and keep him with them.

Chapter Four

The Chin family lived in a small one-bedroom apartment a block away from the restaurant when Chester began elementary school. Chester slept in a small pantry off the kitchen and spent the rest of the time in the presence of Victoria in the kitchen or living room when he was not at the restaurant. A few years later the family moved to a two-story house about a 10-minute walk from the restaurant. Chester liked this much better because he now had his own room. This gave him a little independence and freedom to pursue the things that interested him. But, most of all, it was the fact that he did not have to be under Victoria's watchful eye at all times.

Life for the Chin family revolved around the restaurant and everyone had to pitch in. Even Chester, at the tender age of seven, had to help out on weekends and after school. If there were any family get-togethers, they were held at the restaurant. Since Victoria was not someone others looked forward to being with, there were not many strong extended-family relationships. Even customers saw her as someone to avoid. One day a customer asked a waitress why that lady was always so sour-faced. He said he had been coming to the restaurant for years and had never once seen her smile.

Chester did eventually develop a much-valued relationship with his cousin Joe, even though Joe was considerably older than he. He found that he could talk to Joe about almost anything and not be under the threat of retaliation or haranguing. He was even able to talk to Joe about Victoria. He couldn't understand why his mother was so stern about things. Harry wasn't as cold and aloof as Victoria, but he spent little time with him and didn't seem to take that much interest in Chester's day-to-day life. Chester never got a hug. He never got a smile. He never heard that they were proud of him when he did well at school. This was very difficult for a young boy to deal with.

Hearing from this lively, talkative boy about the difficulty he was having in dealing with his parents' rigid ways, Joe advised Chester, "Your parents are never going to change. That's just how they are. Fighting it will not change them. It will only make your life more miserable. You are better off just to accept them as they are and keep the peace until you can go out on your own." It was wonderful to be able to talk to someone about these feelings and frustrations that were growing and fomenting inside him. Not only to be able to express them but to have that person understand, care and empathize. There were no threats or *you should*'s or *should not*'s. Cousin Joe accepted what he said with honest and sincere concern for him.

Chester thought about what cousin Joe had said for a long time and realized that, although this was difficult, his words were sage advice. He took those words to heart. His parents had given him many opportunities and physical comforts and he was grateful for that. They were not bad people. They just did not know how to express love and caring. There was then, and would always be, a special place in Chester's heart reserved for Cousin Joe.

One of Chester's school friends invited him to attend a Baptist church service with him and his family. They continued to take him to various church and social activities and included him in their family outings whenever possible. This friendship was very important to Chester and he looked forward to any opportunity to be with them. Victoria approved of his interest in going to church because she saw herself as a religious person. For Chester it wasn't so much the religion that attracted him as the chance to be away from his mother's constant scrutiny and an opportunity to experience the freedom and joy of close friendships. He was delighted to see what family life could be like as he observed and shared in the dynamics and fun of a loving family. They talked about things each person was interested in, they laughed and joked a lot and were not afraid to show that they cared about each other. This was a new and wonderful experience for Chester. They would be friends for a very long time.

He couldn't help but think about how his life could be transformed if only Victoria and Harry were even the tiniest bit like this family. He knew that would never happen so for now, he would be grateful to Victoria and Harry for all that they provided for him and to his other church-going family, with the refreshing name of Beverage, for the chance to experience their warmth, fun, charm and caring.

Chapter Five

The family managed to survive for the next few years, but things were looking more hopeless than ever. Food was becoming even more scarce. If food was available it was usually through the black market at a highly inflated price and they had no money to buy it. It was now the middle of the forties and China, still in the throes of war with Japan, was fighting nationwide starvation. Devastating poverty was the norm. Families had to give the government a third of the crops they raised. This left practically nothing for the family to live on.

Little Yick had made it to five years of age but without an adequate diet he was destined to suffer the fate of their two previous children. The oldest of the two girls who had died, lived the longest. She died at six years of age. The youngest had lived to two years of age. Ying was determined that this would not happen again. They must find a way for this youngest child to survive.

He was such a bright little boy with lots of determination. He learned to play Chinese chess at this early age and became a good player. He would challenge the adults to games and frequently beat them. This was his favorite thing to do.

Xu really loved his little brother. Even though only four or five years old, little Yick did all he could to get food for the family. If someone shared a few peanuts with him he always brought them home so everyone could have some. Some of the relatives in the village would scold little Yick for showing up at mealtime everyday. He would stand at the doorway watching them eat. They would finally give him a rice ball and shout a curse, "Eat it and lose your sight!" When Xu came looking for him, he would tell him to throw it away, but Yick insisted on bringing home this ball of rice about the size of a duck egg to be made into jok – a soupy rice mixture – for all the family. One day, as the four of them sat eating this meager meal, Xu, overcome by long pent-up emotion, cried out, "Why must we endure such curses?" It was a time of great frustration and seeming hopelessness.

In desperation Ying encouraged Xu, now in his teens, to leave the country and go to Indonesia where he would have a chance to build a life for himself. Three of his father's brothers lived there and they would help him get a start. He was intelligent and capable but had to give up his education after only two years of school to help work the family farm. Xu had always sensed that in the back of his mother's superstitious mind, in some strange way, the fact that he had survived and the siblings that followed did not, seemed to make of him a harbinger of doom for the family. It was as though his being alive somehow made her more acutely aware of those who were not. It was another strange complexity in the tangle of their existence. Maybe his going would alleviate that for both of them.

During this time hundreds of Chinese were trying in any way they could to leave their hopeless life in China and go to another country. Most wanted to go to America, but it was difficult to get legal papers. Consequently, people would use any means available to get documents, legally or illegally, to enter another country.

In a neighboring village a woman named Chu King Kwai had several relatives who had successfully emigrated to America. These relatives were living in large cities throughout America   Having learned what is required to emigrate, she acted as an intermediary to help others who wanted to leave China. She had a teen-age daughter, Yee Ping, who also went to America   Yee Ping knew a child-less Chinese couple now living in America who told her they would like to find a Chinese child to adopt. When Yee Ping returned to China for a visit and told her mother of this request, they spoke with Ying and Zhong because they knew of the unsuccessful adoption in the past and the ex-tremely difficult conditions in which they were now living. Yee Ping asked 5-year old Yick if he would like to go to America. He bounded back, "Sure!" having no real idea of what that meant.

This seemed to have great possibilities because the cou-ple looking for a child to adopt were people Ying and Zhong had actually known. The husband had lived in a nearby village when he was young and the wife had been a school chum of Ying. Ying remembered her as being kind and innocent. This could be the answer to their prayers. Their child would have plenty of food, a good education and a loving home. It would be a much better life and future for him. The woman had made a promise that the child would stay in touch with his birth family and would refer to his real mother as his "God Mother". She sent a gift of $300 to encourage them to consider the arrangement. The family in turn would receive enough money from the adoption ar-rangements to provide for their food and sustenance.

It seemed like the best thing for them to do, all things considered; but, what a heart-wrenching decision. They would be giving up their child and might never see him again. This thought literally took her breath away as she sharply gasped and then took deep breaths to regain her composure as the tears continued to flow.

Zhong decided he would draw up the adoption agreement himself to make sure that their concerns for their son would be met. He worked with the intermediary in writing this agreement. This was a huge decision for them and it had to be right.

The whole procedure would take time. The couple had to be contacted to define the needs and requirements for the adoption and then, the most difficult challenge would be to find a way to get the child into America if the agreement was accepted. This was no small task. The couple agreed to pay the woman to handle all the arrangements including the expense of getting the child to them in America.

Getting a child to America was a very involved process. Obviously they could not send the child by himself. They would need to find a way for him to enter as part of a family. It would be best to find a family who already had legal papers to emigrate or who had family living in America making the arrangements for them to come.

Reasons for all these strict rules and regulations for entering the United States go back a long way. Huge numbers of Chinese came to America during the Gold Rush of 1849 and even more followed with the building of the transcontinental railroad in the 1860s. They were welcomed because there was abundant gold, much work available and manpower was desperately needed. An immense work force for the railroad project was needed immediately and the Central Pacific Railroad actively imported workers from China for this tedious, difficult and dangerous work. With the authorization of the Pacific Railway Act of 1862, work began during the winter of that year and was completed in 1869. The building of this railroad linked the railway network of the eastern United States with California on the Pacific Coast and was one of the crowning achievements of Abraham Lincoln's presidency. The railroad was completed four years after Lincoln's death.

As the *easy gold* dwindled and the railroad was completed, the country went into a slight depression and the Chinese came to be seen as taking jobs away from Americans. It became difficult for Chinese to enter the U.S. beginning in the late 1800s. In 1882 there were so many Chinese fleeing the rampant poverty and turmoil of war in China that the U.S. Congress implemented the Chinese Exclusion Act of 1882. It suspended all Chinese from entering the U.S. for a period of ten years. The Act was renewed for another ten years in 1892 and again in 1902. The renewal in 1902 was a little different in that this time no time limit was stated - there was no termination date for this Declaration. This exclusion of the Chinese prevailed until 1943 and was then repealed by the Magnuson Act that allowed a maximum of 105 Chinese immigrants per year. During this time it was not only the U.S. that had restrictions on Chinese immigration. Canada, Australia and New Zealand had similar policies.

Although still not an easy thing to accomplish in the mid-1940s, at least the possibility was there. Ying and Zhong and the childless couple living in America would just have to be patient and work with the woman in the nearby village to find a way to bring their tentative agreement to fruition and insure a better life for little Yick. For Ying and Zhong, they must also control the fear and trepidation of giving up their child.

Chapter Six

As a young boy Chester was on a pretty strict schedule. Victoria woke him up each morning at 6:30, then prepared his breakfast. He took his bath every night so all he had to do in the morning was to eat, brush his teeth, wash his face, get dressed and ready for school. His breakfast was always a hot one, never just cold cereal. He would have a full breakfast of eggs, ham or bacon, pancakes or waffles and muffins or oatmeal. Most Chinese believe that the body needs something warm to start the day. A cold breakfast, commonplace for most Americans, would be unthinkable for them.

Another reason for this elaborate meal was doctor's orders. Chester was terribly underweight as a child and, being Chinese, he was already smaller than other children his age. He was not sickly, just very thin, and the doctor said he needed to put on a considerable amount of weight to measure up to his age group. As a very lively, active small-framed child he certainly was not prone to gaining weight. His after-school snacks were things like bacon, liver and onions, and he often had to drink half-and-half milk/cream. Dinner consisted of many types of Chinese dishes in generous portions.

He was expected to study for most of the time after school until dinner. When Victoria was not looking, he would pretend he was a cowboy like Gene Autry, and play with his small cowboy and horse figurines, or he would dream of being a baseball player like Hank Sauer. He was not allowed to have comic books or candy and television was a rare privilege. He was allowed to watch *Howdy Doody* and a couple other similar children's shows if he had done all his homework and there were no more chores to be done. As TV programming expanded, he was frequently allowed to watch *The Show of Shows* and, later on, *Bonanza* in the evenings.

There were many daily chores assigned to him. These chores included helping prepare the food for dinner, washing and drying dishes, and on weekends, he helped with the laundry for the family. Other as-needed responsibilities included dusting the furniture and Venetian blinds, polishing the furniture and washing the windows. Outdoor responsibilities in the same as-needed category included shoveling snow, raking leaves and cutting the lawn. Cutting the lawn was a special challenge because it was not done with a lawn mower. They had a relatively small area of grass, but cutting the lawn meant just that. He had to cut the lawn with a long knife or with scissors. This would be a daunting task for a skilled adult, let alone a six or seven-year old child.

During any free time, holidays or vacation he was expected to help out at the restaurant. His duties consisted mostly of clearing and cleaning tables, filling condiment containers, preparing serving materials and table set-ups and to do whatever else was needed.

In this void of a warm relationship there was one bright

hope. It had four legs and a tail. A mongrel dog showed up in the yard one day who Chester immediately named Lucky. After non-stop begging for permission to keep him, he was admonished that he had to take full responsibility for every aspect of caring for the dog. The one chore he most looked forward to was taking Lucky for a walk. He usually did this before breakfast, after school, and whenever possible. Unfortunately, after a few months, Lucky ran away.

Chester was so sad without a dog they finally agreed to get him another. This time they would get a puppy that wouldn't run away. The new puppy was a well-bred Boxer. He named him Champ after Gene Autry's horse, Champion. Champ was an obedient, lovable dog and Chester's favorite childhood companion. Sadly, it was Champ's fate to be run over by a car as he was racing to meet Chester on his way home from school.

Following Champ's demise they got an older Boxer who, hopefully, would know about not running in front of oncoming cars. Thus, Duke came into Chester's life. Fate seemed to smile more favorably on Duke and, appropriately, brought Duke together with a neighbor dog named Duchess. This acquaintanceship resulted in a puppy named Rex. As Duke was getting along in dog years, Chester was allowed to keep Rex as a pet also. In almost all aspects of a dog's life, this was a pretty good deal. A canine diet here was enhanced with meat from the family restaurant. Whenever it was Chester's job to scrape the dirty dishes at the restaurant he saved steaks or chops for the dogs and got the other waiters or busboys to do the same when he wasn't there. No dog would ever want to run away from such a bounty of gourmet delights!

Chester was very smart in school and always had an answer for anything and anybody. He was thought of as kind of a 'wise-guy' among his peers even in elementary school. This got him into trouble with some of the bigger boys. This trouble was due in part to outright racial prejudice, but mostly to the fact that he was so much smaller than the other boys, and a bit of a 'smart-aleck'. His best friend, Leonard, was also smaller than the other boys and frequently included as a target in these fracases.

In one of these confrontations Chester was struck hard in the forehead with a rock. After that happened, Victoria walked him to and from school in the morning, at lunch, and after school during his first three years of elementary school. This put a damper on the escapades of the bigger boys. Chester wasn't that thrilled with it either because during the entire time there and back she would complain that all this walking was causing painful bunions to develop on her feet and she was suffering greatly. All this because of him.

Chester always wanted to get to school early to be able to play with his friends before the bell rang both in the morning and when he came back from lunch. He had little chance to be with them because he was almost never allowed to play outside after school. He and his best friend, Leonard, used to argue about which of them was the faster runner and whose favorite cowboy was better. Leonard was an ardent Roy Rogers fan and Chester thought Gene Autry was the greatest.

Chester was an excellent student. His favorite subjects were science, math and art. He excelled at history and English, too. He loved to read and could write very well. He especially liked reading animal stories like *Lad, Lassie,* and *Call of the Wild*. He could finish a whole book in one reading at the library and do a book report on it in case it was assigned. He liked to have these things ready ahead of time so he could just hand them in and go play instead of staying in the classroom to do the work.

He was moved ahead a half-grade twice during his first four years of elementary school. He was about to be moved ahead again, but his parents would not give their consent. They felt he was too far behind the other children physically and would have a hard time adjusting. This was a wise decision because he was already a full grade ahead of children his age and very much smaller in stature than anyone else in his class.

Chapter Seven

Zhong, together with the advice of the intermediary, finalized the adoption agreement. Part of the agreement was that the child would be told about his real parents and would be encouraged to keep in touch with them. An amount of money estimated to be approximately $3,000.00 would be paid to the real parents by the adopting couple.

As soon as the document was signed and the money paid, the child would be turned over to the intermediary. The intermediary would then keep the child at her house and proceed to find a suitable method for getting the child to the adopting couple who would also pay expenses during this period of time.

With all the legalities taken care of, the day for little Yick to be taken from his home had arrived. He didn't quite understand what was going on, but sensed that he might not be seeing his mother for a while. Before he was willing to leave, he ran to get one of his favorite wooden Chinese chess pawns and gave it to her saying, "Mommy, always keep this to remember me by." She clasped the pawn tightly in her hand and was never without it until her death in 1971.

It took about seven months for the intermediary to locate a suitable family emigrating to America. The most important fact about this family was that their five-year-old son had recently died. This presented the opportunity for little Yick to assume their dead child's identity and enter America as a member of that family. This would avoid a huge amount of red tape and circumvent immigration quotas. This deception would get the child safely to his adoptive parents without delay. If the husband and wife of the family would agree to say that this child was their son, the adoptive couple would pay them $3,000.00 for bringing him to them in America. They agreed and preparations were set up immediately.

One of the biggest hurdles would be in convincing the adoptive child that his name was no longer Chin Yuen Yick, but was now Lee Gock Keung. He was told this over and over and over and made to repeat it over and over and over. He was also told that he was to call the couple he would be traveling with Mommy and Daddy. They were going to be his parents on this trip to America.

Arrangements were made for departure to America on the USS General Walter H. Gordon leaving for San Francisco on July 14, 1947. The ship would depart from Hong Kong and dock in San Francisco on August 25, 1947. This was going to be a very long trip with only one short stop in Hawaii but they would not be allowed to leave the ship. They would be sailing for more than five weeks in considerably less than luxurious accommodations. This was, after all, an American troop transport ship built to accommodate over 4200 troops.

There were no other children in this temporary family, so keeping a young rambunctious boy entertained and well-behaved must have made the couple feel they were earning their pay. Just keeping track of him was a full-time job. Many of the passengers were seasick during the long voyage and not very tolerant of a young boy's liveliness and pranks. His favorite trick was what might be called a run-by fruiting. He would grab an orange or two and run past the seasick people lying on their cots or out on the deck squirting them with juice. The one thing that did slow him down for a while was that smallpox vaccination. It hurt and his arm was sore for several days.

After arriving in America at the port of San Francisco, the next leg of the journey would be by train. The husband and wife, his parents for the approximately two-month period of transport, were headed to Boston to start a laundry business and most likely, a new family. First, however, they had to deliver this young boy to his adoptive parents. After that they were free to proceed to Boston to start their new life.

Chapter Eight

As Chester grew older and got more of a glimpse of how the rest of the world lived he was becoming more frustrated by all the restrictions placed on his daily life. Not only the restrictions, but the fact that they were non-negotiable. Victoria did not discuss - she decreed.

His friendship with Leonard was a critical part of his life. With Leonard he was free. He could be himself and not worry about repercussions. They could not only talk about all the things important to them but like brothers, they could wrestle and punch each other around and still be the best of friends. Maybe even closer friends for all that release of aggression. They were always punching each other on the chest and arms and no one was really the worse for wear. There was one day, however, that Chester got a little too rambunctious and punched Leonard on each side of his head.

Leonard hollered loudly, "Hey, no fair! You're not supposed to hit anybody in the head! If you're going to do that I'm not gonna play with you."

Chester said, "OK. Sorry. I won't do it anymore."

They reached a kind of 'gentlemen's agreement' that any hitting around the face and head was unsportsmanlike conduct and neither would ever do that.

Some of their friendly bouts got them into trouble. If they were caught playing rough on the playground, it was,

"Chester! Leonard! You boys report to the Principal's Office immediately!"

The punishment meted out was most often based on "let the punishment fit the crime."

Staring at each boy, the Principal would say sternly, with long pauses between phrases for emphasis, "All right, Chester. All right, Leonard. Since you are so good with your arms and fists, you will stand in the center of the room, several arms lengths away from each other, and stretch your arms out straight in front of you. We will then see just how long those strong arms of yours can hold these heavy books." They were required to hold them for several minutes. This was followed by a lecture about fighting on the playground. Frequently, there was a raised eyebrow, tilt of the head and stern look in Chester's direction indicating he was the one considered to be the instigator of these bouts. This always brought a sly, barely discernible grin to Leonard's face.

There were many days Chester had to stay after school for talking too much, disrupting others at study, not following class rules, etc. The usual punishment was to do some pages of math or write a report on a certain chapter to be read. He always had some pre-written reports and math pages that he could hand in to the person sent to monitor him. It was the teacher who usually assigned the 'punishment' but the person monitoring him didn't always know exactly what it was (and certainly didn't know that he had all these pre-written papers ready to turn in). As soon as he handed in what looked like the completed assignment he was free to leave and could go play with his friends.

Victoria was now making frequent walks to and from school again, but not to protect Chester. These trips were for discussions with teachers regarding his behavior, or rather, misbehavior. Needless to say Victoria did not look on all this favorably. She administered her own punishment at home. It was imposed with a seeming non-lethal weapon, a feather duster. This was an implement for dusting furniture made of chicken feathers clumped and tied together at one end of a solid wooden stick. The stick part served as a handle for dusting, but for this purpose it was the handle that was used to apply hard blows to his legs. If he instinctively covered his legs with his hands, both his hands and his legs suffered the blows. He was determined not to let her see him cry or show any weakness. This, of course, only infuriated her more. It also did nothing to make him mend his ways. If anything, it made him feel even more defiant. It was as though those chicken feathers brought out the banty rooster in him.

As he moved to the higher grades, he had a longer school day and was farther away from home. He could spend the lunch hour with his friends at school. He and Leonard had gone all through elementary school together and shared many things, which included being picked on by the bigger boys. They had walked home from school together every day after Victoria's escorting stopped. They would saunter down the long street between school and home talking about kids in their class - especially Chester's first love, that little blonde girl named Jeanette - their favorite baseball teams or cowboy stars and which of them was the best at any and every thing. He stretched those times out as long as he thought he dared. They were so important to him that a little extra time talking with Leonard was worth the 'Inquisition' when he got home. At the end of the long street they parted as Leonard went in one direction to his house and Chester in the other direction to his.

They called out to each other, "See you tomorrow. Get there early. Don't forget to bring the ____."

The "____" would be a comic book, baseball card, cowboy figures or whatever their priority topic had been that day. Chester looked forward to the next day with great excitement for his walk to school with Leonard.

Chapter Nine

Arriving in America after an almost six-week voyage across the huge Pacific Ocean from his home in China to San Francisco, California, in America, there still was a long train ride of several days across the country. Lee Gock Kueng, formerly Chin Yuen Yick, was tired, but excited. He had been handed off to so many adults lately that all this was a bit confusing. He lived for several months with the lady and her daughter who arranged to get him to America. Then for the last couple of months he was supposed to call the couple who brought him to America his parents. Now it looked like he was expected to call another husband and wife his parents. Would he ever be staying with the same people or would he continue to be handed off to other couples again and again? Is it possible he would ever be staying in one place for a while?

Everything looked so different from what he was used to seeing. There were completely new sights, sounds and smells. Everybody looked different and dressed very differently from what he was used to. They spoke differently, acted differently. He saw all kinds of things he had never even imagined and had no idea how they worked or what they were for. There were buildings so tall and wide he didn't think anyone could ever reach the top or even the other side of them.

Everything moves so fast in this new world. Traffic comes at you from all directions and just shoots right past. There are small cars, big cars, huge trucks, little trucks and all sizes in between. How do you ever get across a street here? He was going to have to pay close attention to learn about all these strange new things and this new way of life. There are some really amazing things happening around here. What a strange world! He hoped he could understand and get used to all this. It was all a little scary. You don't what know what to expect next!

How he wished he could tell his father, mother and brother about this. Things were so much simpler back there. Everything moved slowly there. His family would really be amazed at all this. He didn't have to wonder what they were doing because life for them was pretty much the same every day - working in the fields, taking care of their animals and trying to find enough food for their meals.

He got an idea! He could send some money that had been given to him so they could use it to buy food. He would do this as soon as he could figure out how to do this and not disturb these new adults he was with. All these adults he'd been told to call his father and mother certainly have been a bunch of nervous, stiff people! It was hard to know how they would respond to such a request. When he finally got the courage to ask, the lady gave him $10.00, addressed an envelope for him, put the money in and sent it to his parents in China. He thought to himself, *That was very nice of her to do that.* Now they would know that he arrived safely and he knew they could use the money. He felt in touch with them now and more at ease.

A Pawn of Fate

When the envelope arrived in the village his parents and his brother were very excited. It seemed like such a long time since he left them. They were extremely relieved to know he was safe, but something about this seemed very upsetting to his parents. Xu heard his parent's animated discussion, but couldn't be sure what they were talking about. Whenever even Yick's name was mentioned his mother would burst out crying and sobbing. Asking more about him now might make her even more upset. She had even fainted sometimes. Their upset was probably just due to the shock of having received this contact from and about him. He thought it best not to ask any questions.

Ying had never stopped crying since the day little Yick left. To see her crying hard was not unusual. Xu had watched her turn that little chess pawn lovingly in her hand while crying silent tears. Their relationship in those few short years had been a very special one and giving him up was absolutely devastating to her.

The envelope did not contain a letter written by him, only by the lady he was now living with in America. After all, little Yick had not started school, so how could he write? He would be starting school and would soon learn how to write. As his older brother, Xu resolved to write to him as often as possible from that day on. He was sure the people his little brother was living with would read the letters to him until he learned to read for himself.

When he went to address his letter he saw that there was no return address on the envelope they received. How would he be able to send his letters without an address? He knew of many people from the area and/or relatives who lived in America. He would write to them and find out what address he should use to send letters to his little brother. He would first write to an aunt and uncle he was sure would be able to give him that information. They would certainly know. He mailed the letter immediately. It would take a while for the letter to reach them and just as long for their answer to reach him. He knew he would have to be patient. It was lonely not having a little brother around. He needed to know what his new life was like, to be sure that he was okay. He must never forget his real family.

Meanwhile, the way things were going in the village, life was beginning to change for them, too. The communist soldiers were visiting regularly and making all kinds of demands on the villagers. Things were very scary. The villagers didn't know what to expect next.

It was now nearing the end of 1947 and the civil war in China between the Communists and the Nationalist government was in its final phase. The Communist forces were now known as the People's Liberation Army and, under the leadership of Mao Tse-tung, now called Mao Zedong, had gained great power throughout China. They now had over one and a half million troops and had captured huge caches of weapons and equipment from the Nationalists. They were gaining power all through China and had taken over not only the southern part but by now, had taken large areas of northern China which had been the stronghold of the Nationalists. The Nationalist government would soon flee to Taiwan as the People's Liberation Army under Mao extended their power throughout mainland China.

This new ruler of China, Mao, had written three major books in the years from 1938 to 1940 that were the blueprint of Chinese Communism. These would set a new direction in daily life for all Chinese. In these works he wrote about the necessity for the "sinification of Marxism." For Communism to be successful in China it had to reflect the uniqueness of the Chinese. The hard-core Marxism of

Russia would not be successful in China. He wrote about Chinese history and said the previous peasant revolts had failed because they lacked the leadership of the Communist Party. He presented Lenin's argument that revolution would be accomplished in two stages; first to gain the support of the peasants and middle-class, and second to establish a socialist government that was state-owned and controlled. These writings were required study for all Chinese and presented under very strict control through public readings and classes.

Most Chinese knew little or nothing of Marxism and were not accepting of Party discipline. To rectify this Mao set up cadres of leaders he personally lectured and trained in his doctrines. They were expected to study his works thoroughly and train others in the same way. This program was initiated in all the towns and villages throughout China so that everyone would become a strong advocate in line with Party directives.

Every village was required to have a structure dedicated for the visitation of government officials and study of the works of Mao. After a long hard day of working in the fields villagers were required to attend evening meetings to listen to readings from The Thoughts of Mao. Harsh penalties were imposed if you failed to attend or fell asleep during the readings. The readings were to be done with enthusiasm, confidence and dedication. Whether you were convinced of the correctness of the teachings was irrelevant. If you did not perform as instructed, you would be publicly defamed, imprisoned, and very likely, tortured and killed if you resisted in any way.

In early to mid-forties, the last years of the war with Japan, people had flocked to areas of greater safety and stability. Most of these more stable areas were already under control of the Communist Party. Inflation was rising at a staggering annual rate of 230% and the black market was flourishing. The new Communist government was in the midst of an intense effort to modernize the country. The stated purpose was to enable the country to stand up to foreign threats, and build a new culture, still Chinese but modern.

All forms of art must extol the soldiers and workers. None of the classic themes expressed in other countries were permitted. The underlying motto of the takeover was Down with the Old. Temples and shrines were destroyed. Capitalists were persecuted, often murdered. Soldiers of the Red Guard, the elite corps of the army, were taught that violence was the measure of their dedication – this was an insurrection!

The Communist government did place a high priority on education. They built an educational system making primary education available to all children. Programs aimed at increasing literacy for adults were also established. Children were in primary schools from age six to twelve and in middle school for five more years. After all, one could not thoroughly study the works of Mao without an education. Access to higher education was limited, but women's rights were promoted and women began to gain stature in the community as individuals. Many women even became leaders in political actions.

This was the fast-changing life style in the village since little Yick had departed. His new life style in America has drastic changes in store for him as well, but they were bound to be much safer and more comfortable than what was happening in his village of birth.

Chapter Ten

As he grew older Victoria was no longer hovering as much. He had more of a chance to play or hang around with friends after school. He couldn't stretch it too far or he would be getting home much too late. He would have to make up excuses to give Victoria. She probably even knew how many steps it was from school to home. He would tell her that he had to go to the library or help the teacher, or any other reasonable sounding excuse he could create.

As her continual hovering lessened a slow surge of teen-age rebellion began to emerge in Chester. Its focus was on the strict rules and procedures and being forced to study, study, study at home. This attitude appeared with greater frequency, regularity, and intensity. Although his grades were fine, he was becoming more of a discipline problem at school. He was very smart and could do the required work very quickly which made for 'goofing off' time.

All the kids at school had candy, comic books, watched lots of TV, played outside most of the day and didn't have to work at their father's business or cut the grass with scissors! Not being up on comic book characters and TV shows wasn't helping his socializing at school either. He had established a reputation at school for always being up on things and couldn't afford not knowing about all the things the other kids were talking about or doing. He was fascinated with Superman, Superboy and all the Marvel comics that he was not allowed to have. This called for drastic measures. He saw no other way than to occasionally snitch a dollar or two from Harry and buy these things himself. If Victoria discovered any of these ill-gotten treasures hidden somewhere in his room he would just say that someone at school had given them to him.

He was older now and realized that there were not too many more years before he would finish school and, as Cousin Joe had said, *"...you can go out on your own."* Reflecting on this, he did what was expected of him at home, worked in the restaurant, even though he really disliked it, and became resigned to his role in the family. He was pretty much just a typical kid in these years. The only highlights of his life were his continued friendship with Leonard, whom he saw every day at school, and with the Beverage family who took him to church on Sundays. He would spend almost the entire day with their family and frequently into the evening as well.

When he reached high school age, it was a severe blow to Chester that he would not be going to the same high school as Leonard. The district for high schools was not the same as the district for elementary schools. Chester lived one block outside of the boundary for the Lakeview High School District where Leonard would be going. He lived just one block inside the district for Waller High School which was far away and required a 20-minute bus or streetcar ride to get there. He hated both the long bus ride and the school. He felt very alone and was having a hard time making friends. There were a lot of rough kids and people with whom he simply did not identify or want as friends.

Harry and Victoria sensed that this was not a good situation for Chester. They were uneasy about the rough and tough influences he was facing. They decided it was time to buy a house in suburban Chicago on the northwest side and eventually found a suitable house in the northern part of Chicago. This was a nice middle-class neighborhood with excellent schools. Chester was greatly relieved at this decision and felt much happier there. He enrolled at Taft High School. Although he was the only Asian in this new school he felt no prejudice at all. He got along well with everyone and had a chance to be exposed to sports. He hung around with all the various sports teams. Although he was not an especially good athlete, he had great fun being part of the teams. He developed some physical skills and loved the camaraderie. Making the teams was not as important as just being accepted. At last he was part of the crowd.

Chester's high school days were pretty standard. There were no more behavior problems. Although he was highly intelligent, he got only average grades. This was due to his loss of interest in his studies – a pattern that was to continue. He was a very popular student and got along well with everyone. Although he had lots of friends he knew that none would ever be as close a friend as Leonard. After high school, he and these new friends would probably go their separate ways and never see each other again. Not so with Leonard. Although he wasn't able to see Leonard every day like he used to, they still kept in touch and spent time together whenever it was possible. This was a friendship that was not going to go away even if they were in different schools. In fact, they would keep in touch throughout their lives.

That part of Cousin Joe's advice *"...until you can go out on your own"* was now looming. He was certainly looking forward to its arrival! Victoria and Harry had already discussed his going to college and determined that it would be in Boston. They were already telling him who he must visit and spend time with while there. Again, a decree – no discussion. But he was so looking forward to getting away from them that anywhere was fine with him - the farther away the better. Where was not so important. The operative word was <u>away</u>! Still, he would sorely miss Leonard and the Beverage family.

Chapter Eleven

*D*aily life in the village was becoming more under the strict control of the new Communist government. In some ways things were getting better and in other ways they were worse than anyone could imagine. Food supplies were improving, women were given equal rights, and a program of revolutionary land reform was underway, but everyone lived in great fear and trepidation of the soldiers and the new government. Quangdong Province was one of the very last areas to come under tight Communist rule so the level of reform being initiated there was intense.

In this early period of establishing a more modern stable China, the influence of Soviet Russia was immense. It came in the form of expert advice, extensive economic aid, and the introduction of Soviet methods in industrial management and collectivization of agriculture. It was a time of turmoil, improvements, and fear.

Xu, being of recruitable age, had to carefully maintain a role of supporting the government changes in order to protect himself and his family. This became an all-consuming task. One had to be careful not only what you said, but also to whom you said it. Any doubt of your commitment or hesitation to actively participate in the training would bring dire consequences.

Despite these anxieties of daily life Xu persevered in his attempts to get in touch with his little brother. After several months he still had not received a reply from his aunt and uncle about where to send letters to little Yick in America. This was very disappointing. He decided to send the same letter to other relatives to see if they would answer. He waited several more months and still no answer. Well, he would just keep on sending letters to everyone he knew in America. even if it took forty years. Surely someone would give him the simple answer he needed.

Xu still recalled vividly the day little Yick left the village for America. His parents had chosen the time of day for his departure in keeping with their superstitions for his safety, but they could not go to see him off. It was a long distance from the village and they simply could not bear to see their own child leave them. Their sadness was so intense that they feared they would not be able to act in an appropriate way and that, according to their superstitions, would bring bad luck. Xu was the one to take little Yick to the new "parents" for departure on the ship from Hong Kong. Little Yick was gone from their lives before the sun was fully risen. Every detail of this emotional event would be deeply etched in Xu's memory for all time.

He often wondered about the reaction of his mother and father when the letter came that little Yick had arrived safely. They were so happy and then, so very upset. Both his parents had been terribly sad since the day Yick left them. His mother had taken it especially hard. She would break down in tears at the mention of his name and never was the little chess pawn he gave her out of her grasp.

Xu later found out that a short letter inside the envelope

with the $10.00 had said there would be no more letters and no more contact of any kind with them about their son. Any letters sent would be returned unopened. They would not let little Yick even see them. His mother kept the letter until she could bear it no longer and then she set it on fire and let it burn to ashes. The burning of the letter was her final acceptance of the fact that little Yick was now part of this new life they had sent him to. No longer would they be able to know anything about him or he about them. This adopting couple, their friends from childhood, had offered this promise that he would remain in touch with them and they could still be a part of his life. Now no one would give them any information as to where he was. No one who knows about all this would tell them anything! What a bitter realization! What an awful betrayal.

In the next two years Xu, at his mother's urging, left China. He went to Indonesia where several uncles lived and began a new life. In the same year that Xu left the village, another brother, Chin Yuen Ke, was born and three years later, a sister, Chin Xin Yi, came into the family. Xu kept in close touch with his parents and his new brother and sister, but never returned to China. He sent whatever money he could spare to them for food and whatever they needed. His determination to locate his first little brother did not diminish. He continued sending letters from Indonesia to relatives and friends in America asking for their help in contacting him even though he was getting no response from anyone.

Part Two

Chapter Twelve

These new decrees from Victoria about places he must go, people he must contact, stirred some questions that had been lingering in the back of Chester's mind for a very long time. They were about the kind of things he never felt he could question. Since neither Harry nor Victoria was a fount of information and more than unreceptive to being questioned, he had just concentrated on being obedient from the tender age of five. He had gone along with whatever they said, and did whatever he was told to do.

He recalled Victoria's lectures that he was their biological child and they were his parents. These were followed by the caution that, if Immigration authorities or any government officials or anyone outside the family asked about this he was to say that Victoria and Harry were his godparents and he was only living with them for a while. The Lees were listed on paper as his "legal parents" for a reason he never did understand.

As an obedient young child, he just said, "Okay," and withheld his questions.

If he was brave enough to ask anything, the answer

was, "You just do as you're told. There's nothing else you need to know."

All the relatives were close-mouthed at the slightest hint of any question along these lines. If such a comment or inquiry came up, all present would seem to freeze and turn away. With that kind of psychological door-slamming he stopped asking questions at all and, eventually, even ceased being aware that he had any questions.

He recalled that on one of the rare times Leonard was invited to his house Leonard asked him, "Why is your living room roped off?"

Chester's matter-of-fact reply to him was, "Only my parents and their guests are allowed in there."

As he grew older this unfolded as a symbol that there were other areas of life that were roped off, too.

Cousin Joe had been the only adult who ever gave him a sense of having empathy for his thoughts and feelings, but he, too, was just as non-giving of information as the rest of the relatives. He gave him wise counsel but there was absolutely no discussion of individuals, family details, background or history. Cousin Joe told him outright that he understood his frustrations, but that he, Joe, would never say anything against Victoria. Chester had always pondered everyone's staunch avoidance of this subject but knew from experience that Victoria got what she wanted and evidently ruled more than just him with her decrees.

In the days before actually enrolling and starting at Boston University, Chester needed a chance to get used to the area and be able to find his way around. He left Chicago a few weeks ahead of the start of summer school to get acquainted and acclimated. There were certain people his parents required that he visit in Boston. There was the Lee family, of course, and one man in particular who seemed to do a lot of things for the Chinese people there.

His office was in Chinatown. Evidently there was something about Chester's citizenship that had to be cleared up and he was the person who could straighten it out. He didn't know what that was all about or exactly what this man did for a living.

Victoria's father and a brother named Poy, lived in Boston so, of course, they were a *must visit*. Victoria's father, Chester's grandfather, was retired and easy to get in touch with. You could always find him at this grocery store that catered mainly to restaurants. This was where his grandfather's friends either worked or just hung out like he did. You could almost always find him there. Chester liked going to Chinatown to visit with him.

He had a bit harder time visiting his uncle. Uncle Poy did not live in Chinatown. He owned a Laundromat located in a suburb of Boston not too far from Chinatown. It was far enough away that you needed transportation to get there. His business kept him very busy, but with a phone call ahead of time he would frequently take Chester for dimsum on Sundays. Chester stayed at his house several times, too. Uncle Poy always wore a hat. Chester understood why when one day, as they entered his house, Uncle Poy removed his hat revealing his bald pate. He was balding early and wanted to hide that fact as much as possible. Being bald in those days was not an "in" thing.

Chester also found out that Uncle Poy was ostracized from the family because he had married a very good-looking Caucasian woman. "All things Chinese" was the rock bottom rule of this family. Uncle Poy and his wife had a boy and a girl who were, of course, Chester's cousins, but their interests and way of life were not the same as his and they never became close. Chester was trained to do things the Chinese way and these cousins acted and thought about things in a way that he did not understand.

61

He was also required to spend some time with the Lee family. He never was comfortable around them and did not understand why it was so important that he visit them. It was a decree from Victoria, so he complied, but he didn't spend any more time there than necessary.

Chester was finding out more and more that most people in this modern world did and thought about things very differently from the way he was brought up. Even simple basic things like when to shower. He always had to take his shower at night and now he was seeing that most other people showered in the morning or whenever they wished. He had been told that Chinese never eat uncooked vegetables - although he did sneak a salad now and then at the Paris Inn as he was growing up. Here, with these people, raw vegetables were almost preferred. He discovered how delicious medium-rare steaks and hamburgers are.

He also discovered the Chinatown YMCA. It became a favorite spot to spend his afternoons. There were people his age who played checkers, chess, basketball, table tennis and all kinds of other games. Checkers was his first game of choice until he got into some of the chess games. They were going on all the time. He loved playing chess and soon it became his realm of expertise. He could beat any player and would challenge anyone, any level, anywhere he saw a chess game in progress. If none were in progress, he would start one.

After a while, the regulars began to weary of being beaten all the time by this young upstart. So much so that when Chester's classes started and he was not there as often, the regulars turned to playing Bridge. They wanted to play a game that he was not an expert in. When Chester returned, he was quite dismayed to find that no one was playing chess anymore, just Contract or Rubber Bridge. This presented a new challenge he had to conquer quickly. He was soon very good at this. Chess was still his favorite game and the one where he was King of the Board, but he held his own and became quite skilled at this new game of Bridge. There were so many new and exciting things to learn. This was a life quite different from what he had experienced. These new ways were challenging to him, but for the most part, made more sense. There was a freedom to do whatever caught his fancy. Life here was going to be much more exciting and interesting than he had ever known!

Chapter Thirteen

The summer of 1958 launched the first few months of Chester's *out-on-your-own* life in Boston. He attended Boston University summer school and shared a dorm room with two other young men. One was a black student with whom he did not get along too well. He always seemed to be laughing at Chester because of his naivete about the American way of doing things. Chester not knowing that everyone takes a shower in the morning and other such routine behaviors seemed hilarious to him. His other roommate was from the south and a bit more friendly, but several years older and an Army veteran. They had an on-going feud over music. At that time Chester liked only rock & roll (a taste he had acquired over the years without Victoria's seal of approval) and this roommate liked only classical music. They got along pretty well though, and learned from each other. Chester also learned about life in the South and found it quite interesting.

In September of that year his application as a full-time student at Boston U. was rejected. Though rather shocked at not being accepted, he worried most about what his parents might say or do. On the advice of an older student he registered for classes at Newman Preparatory School to make up the deficiencies in his transfer units for full-time enrollment at Boston U. This worked out well and he was successful in these classes.

He moved to a popular rooming house for Boston U. students. He became close friends with two Jewish students who lived next door. They were both from Philadelphia and were attending Boston U. This was another new culture and history to learn about. They cooked some of their favorite meals for each other. Chester introduced them to Chinese cuisine and they introduced him to Jewish and normal American fare. He developed an instant liking for beef cooked rare. Chester shared his love of all the big rock & roll hits, and they introduced him to country & western.

These new friends were serious students. One was studying law and the other was studying psychology. They invited Chester to their homes during vacations and took him on sight-seeing tours of Philadelphia. It was quite an eye-opener for Chester because he had had only limited exposure to much that was not Chinese.

There were so many interesting people living there who loved to have fun. A big pastime at the dorm centered on board games and card games. Between classes there would always be various kinds of games going on in the students' rooms, in the parlors, on the porches or, if the weather was nice, out under the trees. Once he got involved in a few games, it was impossible to quit and these could go on far into the night.

Checkers was the big thing at the dorm. Chester became so good at playing the game that one of the students suggested he go to the YMCU (Young Men's Christian Union) in downtown Boston where he would find really good players to challenge. Besides, it was no fun for them when Chester won all the time.

It became another favorite place Chester found to spend his spare time. Although the name says Young Men's…, most of the members were considerably older than Chester and almost all were Caucasian. It was a quiet place with a smoke-filled atmosphere. All were in deep concentration over their games.

These players were advanced in the game of checkers and offered a serious challenge to this young expert. When they saw that he could rise to their level, they suggested that he try chess. It was a more complicated game and involved much more strategy than checkers. Learning the game from such strong players Chester caught on very quickly, and was able to hone his game to a high level of play. An excellent memory is essential to develop your game strategy. You have to remember from ten to twenty opening moves made by each player. This was exciting and a real challenge.

Chester's experience at the YMCU became extremely important to him. The organization itself also helped him in many ways. Players who ranked as Masters and Experts of the game visited frequently. He became such a good player that one day he battled to a tie game with the reigning U.S. Chess Champion. The organization realized he had potential and helped pay for his membership in the United States Chess Federation. This allowed him to participate in many high level tournaments in which he usually placed well. This was where he expended his energy. This was where his excitement and satisfaction were fulfilled.

All this freedom and exposure to a broader world was so intriguing to Chester that he gave little thought, time or effort to his classes. After all, in his previous schooling he'd been able to excel with a minimum commitment to studying. Why should this be any different?

Having led such a sheltered life with Victoria and Harry he was quite immature about things of the world. It's true that he did have to exercise great control living with them, but that was an imposed control, not self-control. Not the kind of inner control needed to make considered and wise decisions for his life. He was like a bird just let out of a cage - so happy to be free and flying that he didn't ever want to land or pay attention to landmarks or instincts. This was too much fun!

He met interesting girls here in spite of Victoria's admonition never to have anything to do with girls who were not Chinese. Even if the girl *was* Chinese she had to meet further criteria of family, status, just how Chinese she acted, how she looked, wore her hair, walked and talked, etc. Dating was a nerve-wracking experience, not because of being around girls but for the cross-examination he had to go through with Victoria. He dated during high school in spite of her, but it had to be done surreptitiously. Here he could be friends with girls and not feel Victoria breathing down his neck. However, when each summer came he would have to return to Chicago, work in the restaurant, and be under Victoria's watchful eye again.

There was one girl student with whom he began spending a lot of time. She was French-Canadian with an American-Indian heritage. She taught him about manners and social graces and tried to get him to dress a little more fashionably, although that was not high on his priority list. She knew all the board and card games the students were playing and she helped him learn the basic strategies of the various games. They were good friends and enjoyed each other's company.

A relationship like this would send Victoria into orbit,

so he did his best to keep her from knowing about it. She, of course, found out and expressed her displeasure in that unmistakable *Victoria-n* manner. Prior to this she had discouraged all involvements with any kind of girls. He was to study and not get side-tracked! She put a stop to this relationship, but she knew she couldn't stop his interest in girls. When he returned to Chicago for the summer, she made a supreme effort to introduce him to Chinese girls. Her strategy focused on making sure any girls he dated were Chinese and of her choosing.

During these months he also had become good friends with the Director of the Chinatown YMCA. He was a Chinese man several years older than Chester named Henry Chin – no relation to Harry and Victoria. Henry was the best Chinese table tennis player in all of Boston, if not the whole state of Massachusetts. He would take Chester with him to New York City and other locations when he played in tournaments. They would also go other places, such as Cape Cod, just for a relaxing weekend. Henry was single but his life was taken up with the care of his elderly widowed mother, who required a great deal of care.

At the end of his first year away Chester had completed a successful year at the Newman Preparatory School, was rejected at Boston U., applied at Suffolk University and was accepted. He moved to an apartment near the University. It happened to be within walking distance of both the YMCU in downtown Boston and the YMCA in Chinatown, his two favorite hang-outs. Unfortunately, his university classes were last on his list of Things to Do and Places to Go.

At the end of his second year of his *out-on-your-own* life, he had failed his classes and was out of Suffolk University. He was afraid to tell his parents that he flunked out so he made up a story about what had happened. When the summer was over, much to his relief, they allowed him to go back to Boston where he desperately wanted to be.

With the Suffolk U. report cards hidden away, he returned to Boston and knew that he must now try to find a job. He decided to bank whatever money he received from his parents and look for work. He took a couple of part-time jobs. One was with a financial firm and the other as a dishwasher at a Polynesian restaurant. His friend Henry had since left his job at the YMCA and taken a job as a waiter in a Chinese restaurant. He wanted Chester to take a job there also, but the Polynesian restaurant offered him a full-time job if he would stay. His work hours were from evening to closing time leaving his days open to spend time with his friends. He knew this type of life was not fulfilling, but he wasn't sure what type of life would be fulfilling for him. School was too boring. He didn't want to waste the time, money, and effort when he really didn't know what he wanted to do with his life.

At the beginning of 1961, he got up the courage to tell his parents that he was not in school any more and that he was working. He didn't tell them where he was working or what he was doing. Victoria rushed Cousin Joe to Boston to find out just what Chester was up to. Cousin Joe showed up at the Polynesian restaurant unannounced one day and told him that Harry was ill and had had a heart attack. He said that Chester was needed at home in Chicago to help out at the restaurant. Chester immediately packed up and went back to Chicago to work at the Paris Inn full-time. It turned out that Harry was not really as sick as they had made him out to be, but now, here he was, back home with Victoria. How long could he take this?

Chapter Fourteen

Chester's life was in need of some relationships like those he'd had in Boston. The relationships he had enjoyed with his new friends there were important in his life and to his growth. Such relationships were now totally lacking.

His best friend Leonard had joined the Army and wasn't around. It wasn't long before the problem of dating girls came up. The fact that Chester had been dating a Caucasian girl so displeased his parents that they designed an all-out campaign to have him meet Chinese girls.

A Chinese woman Victoria knew had a friend with a daughter about the right age. They conspired to have her friend's son who owned a restaurant invite them all to dinner there. The woman's son could then introduce Chester to the other woman's daughter, Mavis Ho, at the restaurant. Mavis was from Hong Kong, thus Chinese, and spoke fluent Cantonese. Chester remembered how Victoria used to warn him about those 'city people' who were more sophisticated - *tricky* she liked to call them - and likely to take advantage of country people from the small villages. Coming from Hong

Kong made Mavis a 'city girl' thus slightly suspect of being as trustworthy as their people from the Toi Shan area who were country people. Victoria was willing to compromise on this fact though, at least, Mavis was Chinese.

Chester was quite taken with Mavis. She was beautiful, intelligent, and fun to be with. They dated regularly for the next several months. His parents were not overly warm and welcoming toward her, but then that's the way they were toward everyone. Most important was the fact that they did not try to disrupt this relationship. At least something good had come out of his having to leave the life he'd enjoyed so much in Boston and move back to the life he dreaded in Chicago.

The more he saw of Mavis the more he was smitten! Mavis had come into his life in February of 1961 and he hoped that she would be there for some time to come.

On their first real date he wanted to make a good impression. When they passed by a candy store he said, "Let's stop in here for a minute." He wanted to buy her something special. He picked out a beautiful heart-shaped box of chocolates to give to her. He paid for it and as he turned to present it to her he knocked down an entire display of chocolates standing on the counter. *So much for making a good impression*, he thought. He was embarrassed and upset that he could have done such a thing. He discovered, however, that Mavis had a wonderful sense of humor, was very forgiving, and empathetic. He did make a lasting impression, just not the one he had intended. (Mavis still has that heart-shaped box today.)

Since he had come home to work in the restaurant during Harry's illness, Harry was making an amazing recovery. This could only be due to a remarkable healing or the fact that he couldn't take being at home with Victoria all the time either. Anyway, he was back working in the restaurant almost the same as before his illness. This worked out well for Chester because he could set his hours and make sure he was able to meet Mavis when she got off work. Mavis worked for a brokerage firm in downtown Chicago. He rode the El (elevated train) to downtown Chicago and met her when she got off work.

He would take her to dinner and often a movie or they would go back to her house and spend the evening with her mother and her older brother. Mavis's brother was taking courses in psychology so Chester became his favorite target for questions and project research whenever he came to the house. This required a great deal of control on Chester's part because it was ANNOYING. He did not want to offend Mavis and her mother, but his tolerance level for this was rapidly reaching the saturation point.

When he finally did respond to the inevitable questions with noticeable irritation, the next question was, "Do you always get mad when people ask you questions?"

Fortunately his relationship with Mavis was secure enough to weather this storm and, to him, well worth the effort.

Arriving home after his dates with Mavis he was confronted by Victoria standing there like a monolith or huge stone statue. She would castigate him for getting home so late; spending too much money on Mavis with all these dinners, movies and carfare; spending too much time with her; and on and on. Now an adult, he tried ignoring her. That was not easy. There she stood in her usual schoolmarm style dress with that God-is-watching-you-and-will-punish-you-for-your-sins deadpan glare. It was calculated to make him feel worthless, useless and totally inept. When this goal was reached a slight smirk of success could be seen as she turned away. He had endured this without any change in her style since he was a small boy. As an adult he was at least able to remove himself from her presence without fear of the dreaded feather duster being administered.

It didn't take long for both Mavis and Chester to realize that there was something special happening in their relationship. This was going to require some long-term thought and considerations.

For Chester, he had been very happy in Boston even though he was not really interested in college. He had special friends there. They meant a lot to him and had been pivotal in his life. It was becoming more and more clear to him that his Boston life was coming to an end and that he was going to be back in Chicago near Mavis.

He was taking stock of his life and his future: *Should I get serious and give college another try? For a good career you need a college degree. Should I go for a degree? -- in what? I don't know what I want to do with my life. I haven't found anything that really interests me that would allow me to make a decent living. I do not want to work in a restaurant for the rest of my life. That's for sure!*

He finally decided to go back to Boston, enroll in the Boston U. Summer Session and see if he could come to some conclusions about where his life was going. It would give him the opportunity to say good-bye to his friends there and let them know that they were important to him. He enrolled in several math/accounting classes. These should prove useful to any career decision. He met up with his old friends and hung out at the YMCA and YMCU. He passed his classes this time but it was without any enthusiasm.

By the end of the summer session he had really not been able to arrive at any conclusion about where his life was going, but he knew college was not for him, at least not at this time.

He and Mavis wrote letters to each other daily. Before

he left he bought both of them a very fine fountain pen and a bottle of turquoise ink. Each wrote to the other every day using this easily distinguishable color ink. It would stand out in any stack of mail. These letters were the highlight of the day for each of them.

He was also corresponding with Leonard during this time, although not as often and not in turquoise ink. Leonard had worked for a year before joining the Army and was still serving there.

If Chester dropped out of college he would immediately become eligible for the Draft. Maybe he should just join and not wait to be drafted. That's what Leonard had done and he seemed okay with it. But, what about Mavis? He certainly did not want to lose her, but he didn't know if he was ready for marriage either. There were so many things to consider. He made inquiries about the Navy, Air Force and the Army. He never considered the Marines because he had heard too much about how rough it was. Maybe he and Leonard could be together again in the Army. Chester finally decided that he, too, would join and went to enlist in July of 1961. Maybe it would help him get a better handle on his life.

The only concern with his enlistment was his being able to meet the Army physical requirements regarding height and weight. Chester was not a very big person. He was six feet tall so he could make the height requirement. Weight was not so easy. The Army required a minimum weight of 115 pounds.

At the first weigh-in, the recruiting sergeant took him aside, gave him a few dollars, and told him, "Go have a huge breakfast. Drink at least 2-3 glasses of milk, do not pee, and come back immediately after you finish."

It worked. Chester made the minimum weight, just barely, but he made it. He was "in the Army now!"

Chapter Fifteen

Chester spent his eight weeks of basic training in Fort Dix, New Jersey. Army life was a pretty rigid existence, but that aspect of it was not so different from his life with Victoria. He was already thoroughly programmed for *just do what you are told, don't ask questions* and *expect punishment if you don't follow orders.* No warm fuzzies here, either. Basic training was strenuous physically and mentally, but he survived.

To his surprise chess games were played during their breaks. One day, as he walked past the area where the games were going on, a training sergeant called out to him. (This sergeant, unbeknown to Chester, fancied himself quite an expert at the game.) "Do you play chess?"

"Yes, sir, I do."

"Are you any good?"

"Yes, sir, I am."

"Well then, you sit right down here and we're gonna have us a game."

Chester, one who never liked to lose and was accustomed to winning, wiped him out in three quick games. Because the sergeant made such a big deal of calling him over to play, everyone had been standing around watching. Getting wiped out in front of everyone, of course, did not set well with the sergeant. Next day's assignment for Chester: KP (kitchen police) duty. Chester tried to avoid chess from then on and kept himself as inconspicuous as possible whenever the boards were out. The sergeant, however, would send someone to find him or he was sometimes ordered to be there at a certain time on certain days to play chess. Chester refused to lose intentionally as most of the others seemed to do when playing this sergeant. This prowess and pride of his always brought the same next day's assignment -- KP duty. He was grateful that basic training was only eight weeks long and there really wasn't that much time to play chess.

Throughout Army life the highlight of every soldier's day is Mail Call. Every day Chester looked for letters with that distinctive turquoise ink on the envelope. He was so happy to get Mavis's letters. She also frequently sent cookies and candy. These were a huge hit. If one of these delicious packages arrived on the day before Inspection, he and his buddies would stuff their faces with every morsel. If the package were found at Inspection the next day it would be confiscated because it definitely was not Army Issue. The inspecting officers would get to enjoy all those delicious goodies instead of Chester and friends. They were not about to let that happen!

When his basic training was finished in September of 1961 he had a one-week leave. He was able to catch a military transport from Fort Dix to somewhere in Ohio and then took the bus from there to Chicago. He was so anxious to see Mavis. He had not seen her since early May of that year. A week was not a very long time but his parents offered to pay his fare to fly non-stop back to the base allowing him to stay almost an extra day. He thought it was very good of them to do that and he did appreciate it.

When he returned from leave, his stay at Fort Dix was extended another eight weeks for Military Occupational Specialty Training. Leonard had recommended that he sign up for data processing, but Chester didn't think that would interest him. He was a very fast typist. Office work was something that he could do well without a lot of effort and it could be interesting. The other trainees joked, "You don't see too many soldiers carrying typewriters into a combat zone." A clerk typist he became. Of course, clerk typists preferred to be known as the more manly-sounding – Remington Raiders. Remington, of course, was the trade name of typewriters in most common use in the Army. During this time he developed a special friendship with another 'Remington Raider' named Ken.

At the end of this next eight weeks of training, he and Ken were sent to Ft. Benjamin Harrison near Indianapolis. This was much closer to Chicago. They were there for three weeks during which time Mavis was able to visit. Then the three weeks were up and they got their new orders. He would get another one-week leave before reporting to the new assignment. His new assignment was at Fort Ord near Monterey, California. He would no longer be anywhere near Chicago.

Realizing that he would be back in Chicago for only a week followed by an assignment in California and then who knew where he would be after that, Chester proposed to Mavis and she accepted. They decided not to tell anyone yet mainly because Chester wasn't sure how his parents would react. It was something he would have to be getting used to himself. He had no doubts; it was just a huge step to take in one's life and he wanted it to get off to the right start.

When he arrived at his new assignment at Fort Ord he

was very happy to see that his friend Ken had also been assigned there. Chester was made company clerk to the 6th USA Marksmanship Detachment in East Garrison, a separate area of the Fort. This was an elite group of rifle and pistol marksman who were contenders in competitions with other bases. Ken's assignment was in the main area of the Fort. Chester's position as a company clerk also entitled him to the use of a command car to get from his barracks in the main part of the Fort to East Garrison, which was at a distance from the main area.

This was an interesting development in Chester's life since, not only had he never owned a car, he had never even driven a car before. One of the other clerks taught him to drive this stickshift car during lunch hours and whenever they had a break. He caught on quickly. Most of the areas at East Garrison were wide open and on fairly level ground. He practiced every day, several times a day.

After a few days of learning to drive, Chester's Commanding Officer asked him if he had a driver's license.

He replied, "No, sir."

The CO told him, "Go get one."

This consisted of going to the motor pool, signing a paper and – Viola! – you were a licensed driver. You were issued the license with the footnote that if you got into an accident, the repair bill would come out of your paycheck.

Chester continued to practice driving at every opportunity, but driving a stickshift, learning to smoothly engage and disengage the clutch, gears and the gas with the proper timing, took some getting used to.

One week after being issued his license, the CO asked,

"Lee! You got your driver's license yet?"

"Yes, sir!"

"Good! We're going to the Presidio in San Francisco tomorrow."

"Yes, sir..." and, under his breath, *"Oh, my God!"*

Chester was petrified. Sweat began pouring down his brow at just the thought of it. He could probably pull it off reasonably well on the freeway, but - San Francisco? All those hills? Last night the clerk who was teaching him to drive had shown him a little bit about driving on hills. He told him how to pull up the emergency brake, let the clutch out slowly while gently depressing the gas pedal, make sure you've shifted into low gear, and slowly release the emergency brake. This was no easy feat even with years of practice! Going downhill in San Francisco might be manageable, but uphill? An absolute nightmare! Plus, doing all this with your Commanding Officer breathing down your neck while you are in a complete state of panic? Worst of all, there was no way out of this situation.

The trip started out well enough. He arrived at 0600 to pick up the CO. The drive on the freeway went without incident, but driving in the city of San Francisco exceeded all his worst fears.

After numerous killings of the engine and even more neck-snapping starts, the CO, normally a reserved quiet gentleman, could stand it no longer.

"Lee! Do you have a driver's license?"

"Yes, sir."

After a slight pause, "How long have you been driving?"

"One week, sir."

[*Expletive, expletive, expletive!*] "Pull this damned thing over. I'm going to drive!"

When Chester was able to maneuver into a temporary parking area, the CO got out and charged up to the driver's side. Chester, sweating profusely, quickly jumped out. Since the CO was going to drive, Chester, in a nervous frenzy, started to climb into the back seat.

The CO yelled, "What in the hell do you think you're doing? Get up here in front! I'm not going to have people think I am chauffeuring YOU!"

Chester still has selective amnesia regarding the rest of the trip and/or any follow-up. They must, however, have arrived safely back at Ft. Ord because there they were. It wasn't until weeks later that he could bring himself to tell the friend who'd taught him to drive about the trip. When he was finally able to talk about it, they had a hilarious side-splitting time that lasted long into the night. With continued practice and no more trips to San Francisco, Chester's driving skills greatly improved.

In April of 1962 he received new orders that he was being sent to Rhein Main Air Force Base near Frankfurt, Germany. His friend Ken received new orders, too. Ken was shipping out to Korea. Chester would be allowed a one-month leave before he had to report to the 7th Engineer Brigade in Germany. Foremost in his mind was the fact that he would have a whole month in Chicago with Mavis. They might even start making plans for getting married.

Chapter Sixteen

ack in Chicago for a one-month leave, Chester and Mavis had some big decisions to make. It was so good to be back with Mavis again. Her mother had been after her to date other men. To put an end to this constant pressure Mavis told her mother that she and Chester were engaged. Considering Victoria's temperament, it was doubtful that this information had been relayed to her. She would have been taking him to task about it had she known.

There was little delay in Chester and Mavis's big decision to get married before he had to leave for Germany. Besides being madly in love, there also were practical reasons for doing it now. If they were already married, there would be much less red tape in allowing Mavis to join him there. There was one little glitch in their plans, however. Chester would not be 21 years of age until May 14th. Illinois law stated that a male must be 21 years of age to get married although a female could marry legally at 18. They set their wedding date for May 14th - Chester's 21st birthday. This avoided any legal problems. It also avoided having to go into that area of the Lees - Lee Gim Hong and

Wong Shee - listed as his parents on official documents. Any official permission to marry before his 21st birthday would thus, have to be signed by the Lees. He never really understood why this was, but he knew Victoria would never agree to pay for a trip back to Boston to obtain the signature of the Lees anyway, so having their wedding on his 21st birthday solved all these problems and did not rock anybody's boat.

There was little time to make all the arrangements, so they got to work on it immediately. May 14, 1962 fell on a Monday. This would make it difficult for Mavis's co-workers and friends to attend since it was a workday, but Victoria and Harry made it clear that Monday was the only day available since the restaurant was normally closed on Mondays. They were not willing to give up another day's income even for Chester's wedding. At least all the Paris Inn employees would be able to attend as would Cousin Joe and his family, Connie and her family, and all the others from family gatherings throughout the years. Mavis asked one of her best friends, Bernice, to be her Maid of Honor. Chester asked Wah Gim, the son of George Chin, who first hired Harry at the restaurant, to act as his Best Man. Chester's best friends were not in town. Leonard was in the Army and Larry Beverage was away at college, so he chose someone he thought would be pleasing to Victoria and Harry, and Wah Gim was also someone Chester really liked.

Chester and Mavis were married at the Chinese Christian Union Church in Chinatown followed by a reception at a nearby restaurant. Victoria was willing to pay for the reception, but not for a photographer. Chester and Mavis found a friend who had a camera to take pictures of the wedding and the reception. The friend took the pictures all right but then lost all of the rolls of film. Thus, they had no wedding pictures at all except for a couple of Polaroid shots that Chester himself took or had someone else take for him. At least their honeymoon turned out wonderfully. They left immediately after the reception for beautiful Lake Geneva in Wisconsin. It was a charming place with lovely homes nestled along the sides of the lake. They dreamed about how wonderful it would be if they could afford a home in a beautiful area like this some day. It was so peaceful and scenic there, far from the controlling worlds of Victoria and/or the Army. This was a week of peace and delight for both of them as they began their new life together.

As soon as they returned, Chester had to fly to Ft. Dix, New Jersey, to catch a ship to Germany to report on time for his new assignment. It was very hard to leave Mavis. Not only was he heartsick for her, he was seasick during the entire month of sailing to Germany. This was a period he would just as soon forget. As a matter of fact, he did. He did arrive on time for his new assignment, but could not tell you any details of the trip. It seemed that he had become very good at just shutting out these especially difficult times in his life.

Meanwhile Mavis was pretty miserable, too. It is Chinese custom that the son's wife live with the son's parents when the son and his wife have to be separated. Mavis was now to be subjected to the reign of Victoria. Mavis, of course, had a full-time job and returned to work soon after their honeymoon. She was looking forward to a new life away from her mother and getting better acquainted with her new in-laws. The first indication that this was not a mutually welcome venture was that Victoria charged her rent to live there. Mavis accepted this edict, after all, she was working full-time. In the hope of building a relationship with Victoria, she always paid the rent each week in person so that they could at least have that occasion to talk a little. Gradually Victoria made herself unavailable on the day the rent was due, so Mavis would pay a day or two later to be able to present it personally. When this occurred she would find a note on her bedroom door saying that the rent was overdue. When she tried to explain, she was told she could just leave it on the kitchen table on the day it was due and then it would not be late.

Victoria then began to complain that Mavis was turning on the air conditioner, heater or the lights too much and was running up the electric bill. This was followed by judicious door-slamming just as Mavis had gone to sleep at night or when she had a day off and could sleep a little later in the mornings. These door-slammings were very loud, obviously deliberate, and literally shook the walls. There was no possibility of ignoring them or sleeping through them.

What did Victoria expect of her? No matter what she did or did not do, it was unacceptable. Mavis even worked at the Paris Inn during any spare time she had. There she would be criticized for flirting with the patrons if she greeted them warmly or engaged in any conversation. Victoria made negative comments about the way Mavis dressed, did her hair, what time she arrived home from work, etc.

As these incidents escalated, Mavis was becoming totally exasperated. She had, of course, written to Chester about things not working out as she had hoped. He knew very well what she was going through and could only offer moral support. There was no way possible to please Victoria. He was her son and he had not been able to accomplish it.

Mavis had moved all of her belongings with her to Harry and Victoria's. She kept her things either in her bedroom or in the cellar carefully stored out of the way. This included their wedding presents. The proverbial straw occurred the day she found the box containing her cherished and irreplaceable tea set broken into pieces inside the unopened box in the cellar. She had kept this box in her bedroom upstairs. She had not moved it down to the cellar. It was obvious as she examined the box that it had been smashed in on the sides and then kicked down the stairs. She would no longer take this kind of treatment. She immediately began packing her things, called her mother and asked to move back until she could be with Chester. She made some excuse to Victoria about it being too far to travel to work and whatever else she could think of to justify her leaving and moved out as quickly as she could. She made sure to pay the rent for the entire week although she left halfway through the week. She never thought the prospect of living back with her mother would look so good to her. After a little over two months of living with Victoria going back to living with her mother looked to Mavis like the Promised Land.

Chester was now settled in Germany assigned as Officers' Records Clerk in Personnel. His immediate officer took a liking to him and Chester received a promotion to the rank of SP4. They decided that Mavis would come to join him in Germany as soon as she could tie things up in Chicago. Chester rented an apartment in the home of a German couple about a 15-minute drive from the base. He bought an old green Plymouth station wagon that burned a tank of gas faster than you could down a beer. It also did not like to start on cold mornings without considerable coaxing, but in spite of all that, it enabled him to gain some freedom and privacy to wait and prepare for Mavis. The plan was for her to arrive in early January of 1963.

Being alone at Christmas was hard for him. It was freezing cold and he was lonely and miserable. His buddies from the barracks wanted him to celebrate with them. What do most guys do when they are alone and get together far from home to celebrate anything? Chester normally did not drink. He didn't like the taste or smell of beer and/or liquor. His buddies talked him into taking at least one drink. "This is Germany - famous for making the finest beers and wines." Once he got one down (he didn't even know exactly what it was they brought him), another replaced it. Soon it didn't taste that bad anymore. Whatever it was, he mixed it with soft drinks from the vending machine and it was going down pretty smoothly. After a few more, he was getting very drunk and very sick. It took a day or so to get over the headaches, dry heaves, and other miseries that followed this day of indulgence. The vivid memories of the aftermath caused him to swear off drinking for life. A vow he has kept to this day.

Mavis arrived as planned in early January on a night that was one of the coldest of the entire year. With such severe weather the train was, of course, delayed at numerous stops and arrived very late into the night. Chester was waiting for her in the car because parking was very limited and he could only park in certain spots for a short time before being forced to drive to another spot by the German police who loved to ticket GI's cars and collect a few marks in parking violation fines. "Zwei Mark, bitte." Each delay, the freezing weather, and the confrontations with the parking police seemed like a test of "let's see just how much frustration, anxiety and angst you can take."

At last her train arrived and they were together. They would no longer be looking for turquoise ink on an envelope. They could say what they had to say to each other in person – face-to-face – and without delay. This would be the start of a happy life for both of them. And best of all, it would be their life - sans Victoria.

Chapter Seventeen

As they settled into their new home – one small room above the landlord with a tiny kitchen and bath – a mutually beneficial friendship developed with their new landlords. Frau Winter would frequently invite them to dinner and Chester would shop for them at the PX on the base to get American products at considerable discount. Particularly appreciated was American toilet paper. They said that European toilet paper was almost like sandpaper. Among other cherished items were coffee, tea, milk, and ice cream.

He was so happy to be starting a real uninterrupted life with Mavis. They spent the weekends traveling all over Germany. They would often start on weekend trips at 2:00 AM, drive for 6-8 hours, pull off the road and sleep for a couple hours. Then they were ready for a great day of sight-seeing and/or shopping. Since Chester had to report for Roll Call at the base very early (0600) on Monday mornings, they usually had to start back late the night before depending on how far away they had traveled. They didn't care about any discomforts or inconveniences. They

89

were having a wonderful time together and no price was too great for that.

It was several weeks later, near the end of January, 1963, that a letter from the INS (Immigration and Naturalization Services) Office in Chicago arrived. It was addressed to Chester Lee at the AFB address with a copy to the Commanding Officer. *What was this all about?* He had to read it over several times to begin to fathom what it was saying. It stated something to the effect that Lee Gim Hong has confessed that Chester Lee is not his real son, but the adopted son of Chin Moy Kwong, [aka Harry Chin]. Lee Gim Hong stated that Harry and Victoria Chin were not Chester's real parents but did not know who his real parents were.

What does this mean? How does this affect me? He felt his heart begin to race. His breathing was becoming harder and more labored. He sat down and took several long deep breaths. Without understanding the full impact of this letter, he sensed that his life had just been dealt a major blow and he would be facing confusion and confrontations for some time to come. As a soldier he had not been sent to the front lines, but with this letter he had just been sent his own private front line with which he alone would have to do battle.

He thought about his citizenship papers listing his father as Lee Gim Hong. This was part of that whole area of information that Victoria and Harry refused to discuss or even acknowledge. All kinds of thoughts were bombarding his mind. *Since I was a little kid they told me the Lees were listed as my parents in official paperwork, but they, Victoria and Harry Chin, were my real parents. In case of any inquiries by officials, they told me to say that Victoria and Harry were my godparents who I'm staying for a time. They wouldn't talk about <u>why</u> I should say that.*

A Pawn of Fate

Now, according to this letter, is the INS saying that all this is not true? Why is my family name Lee, not Chin, if they are my real parents? Lee Gim Hong says that Victoria and Harry are not my real parents. If that is true, who are my real parents and why did they give me up? How come, with all my relatives around the entire time I was growing up, no one gave me any hint of this? You don't lie on citizenship papers! That's a very serious offense! If what this letter is saying is true, my whole world is turned upside down. It makes me an alien - I could be jailed and deported to China - I hardly speak any Chinese - China is now a Communist country - Mavis is from Hong Kong so she couldn't go to China with me - I lose my U.S. citizenship. This is very scary!!! What is going to happen to me? To us?

Chester immediately contacted his CO about this situation. Throughout the next weeks and months, in trying to clarify his status, he was required to fill out tons of paperwork and make sworn statements over and over regarding his background. He had to give the names and addresses of every place he had ever lived, names of character witnesses, list all the members and relations he knew both of the Lee and the Chin families. He got character reference letters from everyone he could think of who had known him long enough to be able to attest to his good character. Besides all this he was told that the INS had interviewed his neighbors in Chicago and Boston.

Throughout this whole process, his CO and all his other officers were very supportive and willing to vouch for him in any way. They all wanted him to stay in the Army.

He wrote letters to the INS requesting permission to return to the U.S. immediately to resolve this problem. Official responses were slow in coming and when the responses did come, his requests were denied. The Officers continued to support all his letters, inquiries, and applications to the INS. He tried applying for new citizenship papers but this, too, was denied. All his attempts to resolve this crisis were turned down. The end result was that he was going to have to wait until he completed his enlistment in the Army, return to the U.S. to try to resolve this situation, and, "if allowed to stay in the U.S.", he could then reapply for citizenship after the required number of years of residence.

His years of service in the Army would not score him any points either. The INS informed him that all decisions concerning his military status were in the hands of the Army and subject to all Army regulations. One of these regulations had a stipulation that a request to attain citizenship can only be made at the time of enlistment. It cannot be done while serving your tour of duty. In order to re-apply for citizenship he would have to be discharged first, then re-enlist with the stated intention of gaining citizenship. This he did not wish to do with all the uncertainty in the air. If he were discharged then he would no longer be under the jurisdiction of the Army and would then be under the control of the INS. He was not going to risk that even for a minute. He also attempted to obtain a waiver of citizenship for immediate re-enlistment or to extend his time of service. He explored every option he could discover and all were denied either by the INS or Army regulations.

During this crisis Mavis was very supportive and a stabilizing influence for him. They were both in a state of shock with the impact of the letter. At one point she asked him, "Do you actually know who your real parents are?" When they were dating Mavis had heard some things through the grapevine back in Chicago. She had also heard that the Chins, Victoria and Harry, were not his real parents. Because they were newlyweds, she didn't know how he would take such news and was hesitant to tell him what she had heard. But now, with so much being brought into question about his whole identity, she knew she must tell him. It was a question however, that had lived deep in the back of Chester's mind without being brought into consciousness. The more he considered this dilemma, many more things concerning his life came into question.

Chester decided to write a letter to Harry asking him directly if he was their biological son. Harry's reply clearly stated, 'Of course, we are your real parents. Who else would be? Who else would raise you?' Other letters said things like 'everything we have will be yours when we die.' Even though Chester had begun to have conscious questions about Harry and Victoria being his real parents, subsequent letters from them reaffirmed at every opportunity that he was indeed their real son. Not learning anything new from Harry and Victoria he decided it was best just to wait until they came back from Germany to try to deal with this mystery. There wasn't much else they could accomplish from so far away.

After this incredible upheaval in their lives, Chester and Mavis became resigned to suspending the problem until his assignment was completed and they could return to the U.S. There was little choice in the matter. They had done everything they could think of to do as well as everything they had been advised to try, and all had come to no avail. With something as monumental as this hanging over their heads, living a normal life was not going to be easy, but until his discharge in July of 1964, a little over a year away, that is what they were going to have to do. For Chester, uncertainty was no new thing in his life, but this latest one really outdid all the rest.

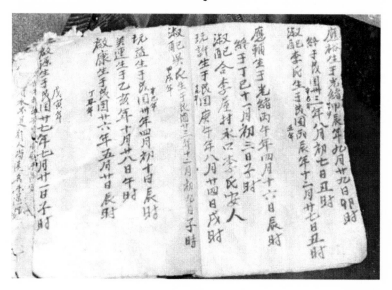

Handwritten Adoption Agreement

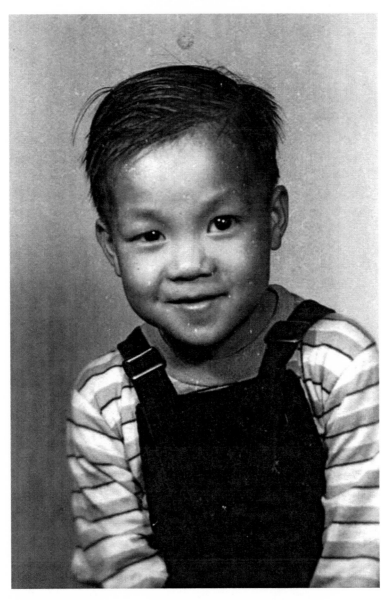

Chester Lee begins Elementary School

Chester Lee with Harry and Victoria

Front: Liu Qiu Ying, Chin Yin Zhong
Back: Chin Xin Yi (Shin Yee), Chin Yuen Ke (Ren Ke)

Entrance to kitchen in village home

Pig sty outside living room of village home

Loft in village home where Chin Yuen Yick was born

Charlie, Chet, and Mavis - 1986

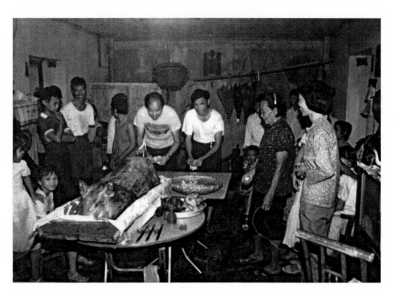

Readying roast pig for reunion feast

The Paris Inn restaurant in Chicago

Chapter Eighteen

Striving to put this crisis in a state of suspension until they were able to take some action was no easy task. In the following months, however, there came some very happy – and unexpected - news to take their minds off the INS problem. Mavis was pregnant! How wonderful! This brought them out of subdued stress and confusion into out-and-out excitement! A baby! This turned their wavering world right side up again. The baby was due in December of 1963. This was exciting news for their friends and neighbors, too. All were very anxious to see this little Chinese baby.

With a baby on the way, they certainly were going to need a more reliable and safer car to drive. The big green machine was just not up to driving mountain roads and was slurping gas like a vacuum cleaner. They sold it to another GI and bought a brand new, bright red, 1963 Volkswagen bug they christened Princess. This was a huge improvement for their trips. Princess maneuvered through traffic like a dream, was great on gas mileage and very dependable. Exactly what they needed. They traveled all over central and southern Germany on weekends or whenever time allowed.

For the next several months, life was to be one long waiting period for monumental junctures to come into focus. The resolution of his status as an American, the discovery of his true origin, and their new baby were pivotal moments not within his power to accelerate. The only thing he could accelerate was Princess and he took advantage of that at every opportunity. Chester decided that a good diversion would be to sign up for some of the Armed Forces chess tournaments. They could combine the tournaments with their travels throughout Europe. These events were open only to the military and a few civilian personnel working at various U.S. military bases. They usually were held at locations within driving distance throughout Germany, but some were in more exotic places such as France and Belgium.

Although Mavis knew the early months of a pregnancy are not the easiest times for a woman to be traveling, she was a real trooper. Driving those winding mountain roads made her a bit queasy at times, but being pregnant it became a constant condition. The maneuverability of that new VW bug was important in getting to the side of the road quickly when the queasiness reached the non-negotiable stage. They made many stops by the side of the road on each trip throughout those early months of pregnancy. Crackers, soda pop and Pepto-Bismol could only postpone the inevitable for Mavis. Once they arrived at their destination and things were on level ground – literally - things were no longer so eruptive.

During some of the tournaments the wives of players would get together to go sight-seeing and shopping. Whenever there were breaks in the matches, Chester would often join Mavis on these jaunts. Mavis was very excited about visiting all the museums, cathedrals, historical sites and famous venues, but Chester did not have quite the level of enthusiasm for these as she did. He needed to concentrate on chess and was glad she could visit these with some of the other wives whenever possible.

Chester and a close friend of his were the best players from the Rhein Mein airbase. Several of the tournaments featured a simultaneous exhibition match with visiting Grand Masters in the game of chess. There were many tables set up in a rectangle for 20-100 players with the Grand Master moving from table to table inside the rectangle. Each board was given a number that was displayed so everyone could know which board the Grand Master was playing against at the time. The Grand Master would start with board #1, make his play and instantly move to board #2, and so on. When he returned to board #1 that player would make his move and the Grand Master would take 10-30 seconds to make his responding move then continue to all the other tables in the same manner. This process would repeat with one move for each board on each round until that game was resolved, usually with the Grand Master defeating every opponent. It would be considered bad etiquette if the Grand Master and any participant were to make more than one move on each round. A move taking more than a minute or two would be allowed at a complicated stage of the game.

At one of these exhibition matches Chester actually defeated a Grand Master who was a former World Champion, Dr. Max Euwe. At another match in Paris, Chester was finally defeated by another Grand Master after all other participants had lost and the only game left was between the two of them.

One tournament took place in West Berlin. Mavis did not go with him to this one. While there he went on a tour of East Berlin. It was a very depressing site. He was appalled at the Wall, the barbed-wire barriers, and bombed-out buildings. He saw a high level of intimidation everywhere and the way people were forced to live under the Communist regime.

Frau Winter told them she had relatives living in East Germany and regularly sent them food packages because food supplies were so scarce there. They sent green bananas (these were very popular because they would be ripe by the time they arrived), coffee, tea, flour, sugar and whatever staples they could manage. When the packages arrived in East Germany, however, some of the guards would deliberately open them, take what they wanted, then mix all the flour and sugar, coffee and tea together before allowing the people to have them. The entire scene seemed grim, lifeless, and threatening. He felt great relief in getting away from there and back home.

Back at home now it was getting close to the time for the baby's birth. They had agreed that it would be best for Mavis to return to the U.S. for the baby's birth so he/she would be an American citizen. Mavis really did not want to go back to Chicago to have the baby. All she could think of was that she would not be with her husband and would have to be with either her mother or, even scarier, Victoria. After long discussions, they finally decided that they would have the baby in Germany and be together. After the baby was born they would go back home and face whatever they would have to face - together.

During these waiting months Chester brought Mavis to the base for doctor's appointments and pre-natal exams. After the appointment was over, they would go to the snack bar on the base for something to eat. As they entered and found a table, all eyes seemed to be on Mavis even though she was obviously quite pregnant. After all, this was in the days of the predominantly all-male Army and a pretty woman was most noticeable. Mavis always liked slices or wedges of lemon with her food or drink, something she did not care for when not pregnant. With great delight she whispered to Chester, "Are they all watching?" She then proceeded to take a large bite of the lemon wedge just as if it were a sweet orange. There followed a community grimace and groan as the airmen's faces turned as sour as the lemon. Chester and Mavis tried to cover their faces to hide their giggles. Why not a little humor with your hamburger? No extra charge!

On December 19, 1963 Kenneth Chester Lee greeted the world in Frankfurt Army Hospital at 0854. After three days in the hospital – not a particularly pleasant stay, according to Mavis, what with Army food, much discomfort, and dingy surroundings – the newly formed trio headed home to assess the considerations this new little person brought to their well-ordered life. With a full head of dark hair and strong lungs to match he brought his parents a challenge neither of them had any experience with.

Frau Winter was a tremendous help and gave them wonderful training in the care and feeding of an infant. Little Ken was a very cute baby and held the fascination of all around him. Especially their German neighbors who had never seen a Chinese baby before and the landlord's three-year-old son, Karsten. He was quite the talk of the neighborhood. Soon those scary he's-crying-what-do-we-do-now times gradually eased into a you-get-the-bottle-I'll-take-care-of-the-diaper routine and all adjusted quite well under the tutelage of Frau Winter.

They continued their travels around the area and took the baby with them. They never went any farther than what would allow them to be home by evening. They had a bassinette that fit nicely in back seat of the car and the baby was snug and comfortable. Whenever they needed her if they were on a longer trip, Frau Winter was a wonderful, willing babysitter.

In April of 1964, when Ken was almost six months old, they had one last chance before Chester's discharge and their return to the U.S. to take an extended trip through Europe. Frau Winter was pregnant and her child was due in June, so she could not take care of baby Ken. They found a good nursery to care for him while they were gone and took this last tour of Italy, Spain, Netherlands and Monaco.

When they returned from their trip it was time to make the preparations for Chester's discharge and the trip back to Chicago. Because he worked in Personnel he was able to make connections on a civilian airline back to New Jersey for his discharge at Ft. Dix in early June. Chester also made connections for *Princess* to be shipped to the U.S.

On the day they left Germany for the U.S., Frau Winter gave birth to a baby girl they named Reno. Mavis was able to visit them briefly before they left for the airport.

Chester, Mavis, baby Ken, and Princess were reunited in New York. They spent time visiting some of Mavis's relatives who lived in the area, saw the New York World's Fair, and then began the 900-mile drive to Chicago. Along the way they made a few side-trips for scenic and historical points of interest including Boston and other important cities. They were not looking forward to facing Harry and Victoria and the monumental INS-inspired mysteries of his citizenship, identity, and heritage.

Chapter Nineteen

A rriving in Chicago near the middle of June 1964, they did not want to live with either family. Not even just until they could get established on their own. They stayed in a motel for a couple weeks while Mavis went apartment-hunting and Chester began job-hunting. He applied for jobs at two banks and received offers from both. One of the banks offered him a position in their International Department. This seemed more interesting to Chester, even though the other bank offered a little more money. He made the decision to go with working in the international arena. Later on, he found out that he was offered the International position because they assumed that he spoke and read Chinese fluently ...which, in fact, he did not. It worked out fine, however, and he remained with that bank for a couple of years.

It took about a month to get settled with Chester's new job and their apartment before they felt up to taking on the families. They had, of course, been in contact and had visited briefly with both of their families. There was a much more relaxed relationship with Mavis's family than with

Chester's. Mavis's mother, Esther Wong, understood that they were just getting established as a family and didn't have much money, so she frequently took them out to dinner. She was not one who liked cooking and preferred to take them out to restaurants rather than try to prepare food at home. Mavis had a sister and two brothers. Only her youngest brother, David, was still living at home. The others were pursuing their careers in other areas of the country.

Chester got on well with all Mavis's family and they liked him. Esther would say that she thought she and Chester were a lot alike. There were strong differences, however, even though their names did sound similar, Chester – Esther. Chester was a very punctual person and Esther was habitually late for everything. She did improve in this regard after they 'left without her' a time or two when there was no other choice. Esther spoke Cantonese with Mavis and felt that Chester was woefully lacking in this skill since he only spoke English with her. One day she said to Mavis, in Cantonese, "Chester has a very skinny ass" and was surprised to hear him reply, "It's not that skinny!" She said, "Oh! You understood that?" and they had a good laugh. The relationships with both their in-laws were quite a study in contrast.

Victoria's birthday was in July. They attended a big party for her at the house where Chester had grown up. All the relatives came to the party, too. It was good to see everyone and they enjoyed seeing little Ken. The new family visited several other times at Harry and Victoria's house with Cousins Joe, Connie and other relatives joining them.

Subsequent visits with only Harry and Victoria and no other relatives present, however, became quite intense and volatile. These usually led to discussions about Chester's citizenship and whether or not he was their real son. Harry and Victoria held fast to their story, but it was becoming clearer to them that Chester had serious doubts about their story. They, however, repeatedly refused to answer any direct questions about his background.

Harry and Victoria were entirely focused on their plan for their retirement, that as soon as he was out of the Army he would come back and take over the Paris Inn restaurant. This was standard operating procedure in a Chinese family. The big problem with this scenario was that Chester hated the restaurant and wanted no part of it, let alone the entire responsibility for it. He did not have the temperament for dealing with the problems of either employees or customers. Working there all his life he had seen that employees would simply not show up for work due to a hangover or a particularly good run at gambling or any other personal excuse that might arise. They would help themselves to the best cuts of meat and other supplies and thought nothing of it. He was appalled at this. Neither did he like dealing with customers or suppliers with their problems and complaints.

He said, "Why don't you just sell the restaurant, take the money and enjoy your retirement?"

They responded, "We do not need money! This is for you to carry on our heritage."

He tried to explain to them that he was not cut out for that type of business and would not be successful at it. The discussion got quite heated and they were simply at loggerheads. Chester rose up from his seat on the sofa with baby Ken sitting on his shoulders preparing to leave. Victoria rushed over and pushed him back down. This shocked him and he was furious that she would do such a thing with the baby on his shoulders. What if he had fallen and Ken was hurt? He yelled at her about all that could have happened to the baby.

Harry and Victoria both shouted at him, "You will get

nothing from us."

To which he replied, "I never wanted your money. I just wanted you to retire and enjoy life."

Chester and Mavis left immediately with the baby. They were very angry. This incident seemed to sever the relationship from both sides forever. From this point on, neither side had any desire to see the other and he was officially disowned by them.

In July of 1965, Harry and Victoria sold the restaurant to Wah Gim. They moved to San Francisco and lived in the Chinatown area. This information was given to Chester later by relatives.

After some time had passed he did try to communicate with them through a few letters. He was, after all, grateful for the opportunities they had given him and he did care about them. He just couldn't take their unyielding insistence on continuing to control his life. It was only Harry who occasionally responded but now signed the letter "Harry" rather than the usual "Dad".

NOTE:

In September of 1966, Cousin Joe informed him that Victoria had died. Throughout her entire life, she had never shown any signs of ill health while Harry seemed always to be ill and was known to have a bad heart. Everyone assumed that Harry would be the first to go. Chester made arrangements to attend her funeral with Cousin Joe and Connie. Chester wanted to reconcile, at least to some degree, with Harry. He had hope of this because Harry seemed to be the more reasonable of the two.

During the services, Chester tried to offer comfort by holding Harry's hand but Harry rejected his attempt. At the end of the funeral services Chester approached Harry hoping to speak with him, but Harry pushed him away. No further contact was possible as Harry refused to respond to any letters from Chester. About 15 months later, again through relatives, Chester found out that Harry had died in Hong Kong. He had died on his wedding night of natural causes.

Chapter Twenty

After Chester, Mavis and baby Ken were established back at home in Chicago and the demise of the relationship with Harry and Victoria was behind them, it was time to pursue his citizenship problem with the INS.

He made numerous calls and visits to the INS offices that, fortunately, were near the bank where he worked. It was not easy to explain his situation to the INS gatekeepers since he was now a man without a country. The questions from receptionists to determine what forms, information packets, and appointment settings would be assigned were based on such prescreening questions as:

Receptionist: "You want to apply for U.S. citizenship, Mr. Lee?"

Chester: "Yes, that is correct."

Receptionist: "Are you now a citizen of China?"

Chester: "No, I am not."

Receptionist: "Then what country are you a citizen of, Mr. Lee?"

Chester: "I am not a citizen of any country right now.

My wife was born in Hong Kong so she has British citizenship; my son was born in Germany but has British citizenship through his mother. I have lived in the U.S. since I was five years old and served in the U.S. Army. Then my U.S. citizenship was taken away due to some confusion about my background of which I know nothing.

This usually required the calling in of a supervisor, discussion behind the scenes and the usual – "Have a seat, Mr. Lee, and someone will call you. NEXT!"

Mavis had applied for citizenship before, but now had to start all over again because she had lived out of the country during Chester's service in Germany. They were both starting from scratch but Mavis's application was not so complicated a situation. In fact, it fit well into standard procedures. Chester's situation required special investigations, records search, review of affidavits, and carried the possibility of deportation. All applicants were required to live in the U. S. for at least five years without leaving the country for any extended length of time. That would make it 1969 or 1970 before their requests for citizenship would be granted.

Chester appealed the deportation issue on the grounds that he had not know any life other than life in the U.S., he did not speak Chinese with any degree of fluency, and it would impose a severe hardship on his family. Mavis could not go to China with him were he deported because of the political situation between Hong Kong and China. It would break up the family. The INS accepted these arguments and blocked any consideration of deportation. This news was received with immense relief, needless to say. Later on, in 1965, the Immigration and Nationality Act was passed repealing the national origins quota system and gave priority to family reunification. It finally came down to the fact that the investigation was complete and Chester was free to pursue citizenship just the same as any other applicant. With the wheels of citizenship slowly moving down the track and the stress of Harry and Victoria trying to control of their lives removed, they were becoming their own entity. Leonard, Chester's best friend from childhood, had returned home from the Army and they could resume their friendship. Leonard had also gotten married. His wife's name was Sue and they had a daughter, Dianna, about the same age as Ken. Leonard and Chester had briefly been in contact while in Germany. Sue's father was a career Army man stationed there. That was how Leonard and Sue happened to meet. Now, back at home, not only could Leonard and Chester renew their long friendship, it was expanded into family relationships as they spent birthdays and holidays together. They got together a couple times a month at each other's houses for dinner and board games.

The first time they got together for dinner, it was at the Lee's. Sue seemed a little nervous as the evening began. They assumed that it was due to getting to know them and wanting to make a good impression. Months later, Sue confessed to them that before that night, her only experience with Chinese food was eating chop suey and she hated it. She didn't want to come to dinner because she was afraid of offending them if she didn't eat what was served. After all they were both Chinese, so what else would they serve? Leonard told her to just move the food around on her plate with a fork and pretend to eat it. Chester was his best friend and he really wanted to spend the evening with them. Sue mustered her courage and went along in spite of visions of chop suey consuming her. To her great surprise and delight Mavis did not serve chop suey! She served a dish Sue had never tasted before. It was lasagna and it was delicious! Sue had several helpings of it. She got the recipe from Mavis and later served this wonderful "Chinese food" – lasagna – again and again at their house. They all had a good laugh which was repeated many more times in telling friends about that first get-together.

These were much happier times for all. Sue and Mavis became good friends, too, almost like Chester and Leonard. Sue served as a character witness for Mavis at the Immigration Office when she went for her citizenship test. She was very proud to do this for her. Chester and Leonard picked up where they left off years ago and for another ten years or so, they and their families did most everything together.

During these early years came another blessed event in the Lee family. On August 2, 1966, a new member, Dennis Lee, joined the family. He was born in Chicago's Edgewater Hospital. Dennis was a surprise in the fact that they just expected that their next baby would be a girl. They had many girls' names picked out and had only given a few passing thoughts to names for a boy. They liked the name Dennis but had no other they liked for a middle name, so Dennis was named Dennis Lee with no middle name. He was a very cute little guy, a good baby and an exciting event in their lives. It was quite a change to have two babies to look after instead of one, but they adjusted well and were fascinated with the new little man in town. Chester tried to notify Harry and Victoria of Dennis's birth but never got any response, nor did they ever see Dennis.

Chester also renewed contact with the Beverage family during these years. They visited them frequently with the two little boys. Larry, Chester's friend in elementary school who invited him to their church, told him later that his mother said, "I can't believe those two little boys are Chester's! They are so well-behaved and Chester was so impish when he was young."

A Pawn of Fate

As the year 1970 began, Mavis received notification from the INS that she had passed the test and completed all the requirements for citizenship and was to report for a swearing-in ceremony at the Cook County Court Building on April 1, 1970. This was very exciting news! She could hardly wait to tell Chester, but then wondered, *where was his notification?* His application was complicated and was sure to take longer, but it was not long before his notification came in the mail. His swearing-in ceremony was scheduled for May 1, 1970.

Although he had lived in the U.S. far longer than Mavis, she got her citizenship first. A detail she could always bring up in any of those husband/wife discussions for a little one-upmanship. All their friends and family congratulated them. Chester's friends at work took him to lunch to celebrate and Mavis's mother took them to dinner for a quiet celebration. It was a very big milestone! They were now undisputedly American citizens and they belonged here in the U.S. They could vote and had the same rights as everyone else. For Chester, he had thought that once before and it all came tumbling down, but he felt confident this time because he knew what was going on, had taken care of things himself, and felt secure.

At this time two of the biggest mysteries to be dealt with when he returned home from the Army were settled: he had his citizenship back, and Victoria and Harry were no longer involved in his life. There was still that third nebulous mystery about who were his real parents. But, that wasn't so critical right now and, besides, he had no idea where to begin with that one.

Chapter Twenty-one

During the next several years, Chester became deeply involved in working with computer systems. Many hours had to be put in on weekends to have new programs and hardware installed and operating reliably and/or systems updated without disrupting the regular workweek procedures. This required long hard hours. Having established himself as a very astute programmer, he was hired as the Systems Programming Manager for several different companies he worked for throughout this period. He made numerous business trips across the country and, as often as possible, took the family along. Even with this intense work schedule he went back to night school and in 1977, obtained a bachelor's degree in computer science from Roosevelt University.

In keeping with their love of travel they took several extended vacations often combined with Chester's business trips. They drove to their destinations whenever possible because they loved to see the countryside and be able to stop when they saw something that interested them. Mavis's mother, Esther, went with them on many of the trips, too. They were now traveling family-style in a station wagon that could accommodate all the people and baggage needed on such trips. They had definitely outgrown "Princess."

One of these vacation treks was particularly unforgettable. They set out to drive to Orlando, Florida from Chicago. It was February, and they almost made it as far as Remington, Indiana, a distance of about 200 miles, when a sudden blizzard struck. It was one of those biggest-of-all-time blizzards. Cars and trucks were stranded all along the highways. They had to walk several miles in the swirling snow to reach shelter at a motel called the Remington Inn. They were marooned there for two days, slept on the floor, and lived on donated hamburgers from a stranded MacDonald's supply delivery truck until the storm subsided and roads could be cleared. It was reported later that cattle had frozen to death in a truck stuck on the road in that storm. They gave up on this being a family trip and drove back home. Since it was a business trip Chester flew on to Orlando and took care of business.

For the most part Mavis was a stay-at-home mom. She took creative arts classes in flower arranging and stained glass for some diversion. As the boys grew older, she took computer-programming classes and showed a real aptitude. She was hired full-time as a programmer in 1977 and it developed into a life-long career.

The boys' interests and personalities were showing strongly by now. Dennis, the youngest, was the more adventurous and aggressive of them. Both boys took judo classes. Dennis especially enjoyed using what he learned in the classes with friends. As an extremely active child, he suffered a broken leg jumping out of a swing at the height of its arc. Ken was the more studious and creative type. He enjoying reading books, studying music and could always negotiate the better end of trading toys, etc. with Dennis since he was, after all, two and a half years Dennis's elder.

Chester was involved with the boys in the YMCA Indian Guides. They were Big Bear, Little Bear and Littlest Bear. When they bought their first house they had great basketball games on the driveway. Another exciting event was going for a ride with dad on the riding mower. (Yes, a riding mower – a bit of a switch from Chester's childhood job of cutting the grass with scissors.) They built a beautiful rock garden and a huge deck that made their house stand out on their street.

There was another member of the family, although this family member had four legs, a long tail, and, whose back, when standing on all fours, was at the height of the boys heads. Meet Duke, the Great Dane. Duke was a character and brought them many a memorable moment. He had the run of their big chain-link fenced yard and often presented Mavis with trophies such as dead garden snakes and assorted other gifts. When meeting people at neighborhood stores or introducing themselves they were always recognized as the family with either the rock garden, huge deck, or Duke.

After Chester had worked at the bank for over a year he was transferred into Computer Operations. This was in the mid-60s when computer applications were becoming the way to go for businesses of any size. This was of great interest to Chester. So much so that 18 months later he changed jobs to become a Programmer Trainee at another large company. This was an entirely new field to him and he felt that everyone else there knew so much more than he. After a year of training at this firm, he was offered another job at a large book publishing company. Here he found that with his previous experience he was considerably more computer savvy than many of the other programmers even though they had more experience in the field than he did.

As he began this new job at the publishing company his project leader asked him, "Do you prefer being called Chet or Chester?" Giving it a quick thought he replied that he would like being called Chet. From then on he was Chet Lee to all his new acquaintances. Mavis liked it better, too. He mentioned to all his old friends and family that he was called Chet at work and he had, indeed, come to prefer it. This seemed to fall on deaf ears because to this day, to them, he remains Chester.

This new career in the field of computers seemed to be his niche. He picked up quickly on the logic of it all and had the right analytical sense to figure out what sequence of steps had to be in place for a particular function to occur. He seldom made the same mistake twice remembering why it was that certain things did not work, as well as why others did. This was not unrelated to his ability to remember what chess moves had been made and what ones needed to be made for a checkmate. All those hours of playing chess, it would seem, enhanced the skills needed for a successful career in this rapidly developing field of computers.

Chicago winters were beginning to bother Chet. He was having neck problems and sometimes could hardly turn his head. This was probably due to sitting at a computer all day with air-conditioning blowing down on him. All computer rooms had to be kept extremely cool with circulating air for them to function properly. Even though he could get away from it for short periods of time, it still was a problem. Outside was the fierce cold and wind of a Chicago winter. The 1977-78 winter was the proverbial straw for him. With the chill factor – determined by the wind blowing off the freezing lake water and the once-in-a-lifetime heavy snow – the temperature reached a bone-chilling minus 100 degrees.

A vivid example was the day he did not park the car in the garage. When he came out the next morning it would not start. He had to lift the hood and loosen one of the nutwing bolts on the radiator to pour in some anti-freeze and de-icer. It was so cold that he could only have his bare hand exposed for a few seconds before having to warm it inside his coat pocket. Frostbite was a serious consideration. When he finally accomplished getting the de-icer in the radiator he had to jump-start the car. All this was performed surrounded by snow and ice in a freezing wind. His "skinny little ass", as Esther so succinctly put it, had about had it! He wanted to move to a more moderate climate. The family vote was 3 'nays' to 1 'yea' with Chet being the only 'yea'.

Chet had gained a reputation as an extremely capable hands-on Systems Programming manager. Other companies wanted to interview him for positions with them. He had interviews set up in Texas and Northern California. None of these really seemed right for him. Then, one day, a call came from Woodland Hills in Southern California. It was from a company that specialized in computer printers and related products. He knew from the start that this was the job for him. He was so confident about it that he brought Mavis with him on the trip for the interview. He even set up an appointment with a real estate agent in the area to begin house hunting.

They arrived on a Friday evening and were met at LAX airport by the man he would be interviewing with. He took them to a nice restaurant for dinner and did the technical interview during dinner. It turned out that he was also the man Chet would report to if he took the position. They hit it off and the interview went well. The company made him an offer the next morning, they did some negotiating, and

Chet accepted the position.

The process of finding a house involved a bit of sticker-shock. Their house just outside of Chicago was almost 2800 square feet on a ½ acre of land that Chet believed would probably sell for around $80,000.00. He figured that he would probably have to 'bump up' to $100,000 for a house like that in California. After the agent showed them what $100,000.00 would buy, that "bump" became a cata-pult. Of course, wages were higher out here so Chet would be making a better salary. Ken was doing so well with mu-sic lessons that they had to have a house that could accom-modate a grand piano and Dennis needed room for all his activities. They would not skimp on good schools and neighborhood. They did find one that they really fell in love with, had everything they needed and was close to Chet's work. They made an offer to buy the house on Sat-urday night and met the agent for breakfast on Sunday to sign the final paperwork. They were now California home-owners at the catapult price of $130,000.00. In the 1970s this was a lot of money – especially for a considerably smaller house and yard.

All the above life-changing events took place in the space of one short weekend in June of 1978. When they ar-rived back in Chicago late Sunday night, their heads were swirling at all the changes to come. As they drove home from the airport, all that happened and all this would entail was running wildly through their minds. They were hop-ing they did the right thing. As they stopped at a red light, they glanced out the window at a fire hydrant they had passed thousands of times before and for the first time no-ticed the imprint of the manufacturer's name which in-cluded the company location – San Fernando. Woodland Hills, CA, where they would be living, is located in the San Fernando Valley. They took this as a reaffirming sign.

They made arrangements to put their Chicago house on the market and Chet flew to California to start his new job. The house sold in one day! It took a few months before the escrows closed on both houses because of the contingency agreement. The bank in California was reluctant to recognize the sale in Chicago until it was completed. The Chicago house had to close before the final paperwork was signed giving them the Woodland Hills house. It was now, "California, Here We Come!"

Chet had been able to go back to Chicago at least twice during this time. That was part of the agreement for employment. He took lots of pictures of their new house, the schools they would be attending, and the neighborhood in general hoping to assure them that the move would be just fine for them.

It was in August that the moving van came, packed up all their belongings and they all began the trek to California. The family drove rather than fly since they liked to travel by car anyway. They didn't rush and took time to visit interesting places along the way. Their family was a little smaller now since Duke had to be put to sleep a few months prior. Sadly, Great Danes are not long-lived. It seems that seven to eight years is the maximum for these wonderful big friends.

They were also leaving almost life-long friends and family. Leonard referred to Chester, in friendly fashion, as the "traitor" for breaking up their great get-togethers. Many things were going to be changing in their lives – again, but these changes were very exciting and promising.

Chapter Twenty-two

It was near the latter part of August, 1978 when the travelers arrived at their new home in Southern California. They took time to see the Grand Canyon, the Petrified Forest and other points of interest along the way and were now ready to face unpacking and settling into their new house, neighborhood, schools, jobs, and friends.

The boys adapted quickly and were made to feel very welcome by several boys their age who lived in the neighborhood. This was a great relief to Chet and Mavis and a big factor in their settling into a stable, satisfying way of life. It was only a few weeks until school began. Things go much smoother when you have friends who know their way around and can help you get acquainted when starting at a new school. Ken and Dennis were fortunate in this regard.

The weather was heavenly! No worry about frostbite here. All the closets full of warm clothes and coats were not likely to soon, if ever, see the light of day. And, as a final touch, a memorial snow shovel was enthroned on the wall of the garage.

It was while watching the Rose Bowl game on TV on January 1, 1979 that they had that inevitable 'Welcome to California!' experience - their first earthquake. It was a 5.2 magnitude, centered deep under the ocean off the coast of Malibu. Damage was slight because of its depth and being off-shore. It did, however, set their nerves on edge and was a pretty good initiation for them by any standards. When it happened Chet's first thought was that the boys were playing football outside and had hit the house. On the plus side, by the time they figured out what it was, the earthquake was over. It didn't last long – only a few seconds. Even though there were some aftershocks of lesser magnitude, on the whole, it just gave a good jolt and was over.

Chet's job was going well. After 4 or 5 months his boss left the company and Chet was promoted into his position as Technical Support Manager. Company upper management wanted to implement new Operating System software quickly even though the department was not ready for such rapid moves. This necessitated many long hour days and weekends to accomplish the management goals with endless phone calls in the middle of the night.

With the boys pretty well grown and in school, Mavis decided to seek employment. She was hired as a Programmer Analyst and later promoted into Technical Support at a computer company just down the street from where Chet was working. This was convenient in many ways. Not only were they working physically close, their type of work was closely related. Mavis was fairly new to this area and Chet was able to give her a lot of support and insight. The computer environment at the two companies was very much alike so they shared a lot of similar problems and solutions. At times the staff at Mavis's job would call on Chet's expertise for help when he came to her office to pick her up and Chet was glad to give it. Mavis was a very fast learner and with Chet's earlier help in learning computer languages, she rapidly became a valued employee. Since the phone in their bedroom was on Chet's side of the bed, he would often answer calls coming in during the night many times unaware of which company had called.

After living in their new neighborhood for several months they realized that they were living in more of an up-scale area than they thought. The boys were coming home from school with stories about a 16-year-old girl who was very angry with her parents. She cried that she was embarrassed to be given a new 280-ZX for her birthday when all her friends had Mercedes or BMWs. Another friend mentioned to his parents that he thought photography might be kind of interesting. They immediately bought him an expensive camera outfit. Within a week it was relegated to the bottom of his closet floor with smudge marks all over the expensive lenses because he didn't want to learn how to use it.

This was not the value system by which the Lees lived or wanted their children to live. It was a challenge to maintain their values in the midst of such a throw-away world. When Ken wanted a stereo he had to earn the money to buy it and was responsible for any care and maintenance required. This applied for any toys either of the boys wanted. Birthday and holiday gifts were never lavish, but were thoughtfully purchased according to the boys' interests. The boys had paper routes and worked at fast food restaurants. They saved their hard-earned money to pay for things they really wanted and consequently appreciated them more.

All this made Chet mindful of the conservative tone of the Midwest where he grew up. This brought to mind

Cousin Joe, Connie and his other friends and relatives   in Chicago.   There was a distance that had developed between Chet and his cousins besides the geographical one.   Connie didn't return phone calls from either Joe or Chet.   He and Joe did remain in touch.   They had not gotten together since Harry and Victoria moved to San Francisco.   He was very angry at the whole clan.   Their reluctance and refusal to give him any help in solving the mystery of his past finally got to him and he no longer wanted to pursue a relationship with them.   If he went back to the area on business, he might give Connie or Joe a call and maybe go to dinner with them, but they still would not discuss anything on the subject of his past.   Outside of that, they exchanged Christmas cards and that was about it.

They kept in touch with Leonard and Sue, the Beverages and a few other friends, but distance and time made their contact less frequent.   Ken kept in touch with Dianna, Leonard and Sue's daughter, but Dennis did not have close ties with friends when they moved, so he didn't care much about keeping up relationships.   Overall, the people in their past were just that – people in their past.

The one exception was Mavis's family, especially her mother.   They had kept in close touch with her and in 1980 discussed with her the idea of her moving to California to live near them.   She was agreeable to this when they presented the idea.   She had visited Southern California and had other relatives in the general area.   This seemed like a good thing for her.   By 1981 they had bought a duplex for her in the area.   She even contributed some of the money for the down payment.   They drove back to Chicago in August of 1981 to help her get things ready for the moving van.   This project emphasized another area where Esther and Chester greatly differed.   Esther was a veritable pack rat and had saved every scrap of paper imaginable.   She had hundreds of boxes stacked to the ceiling in the basement. Much of it was moldy from flooding and age. They worked quickly to save and organize important things like tax records and such, but it was a difficult job. They were also going to drive her car back so she would be able to get around. Ken was now old enough to drive, so they alternated driving the two cars between the three of them to get her and her belongings to California.

Chet took his three weeks vacation time for this trip. He also had given notice at his job and was to start a new job with a mortgage company when they returned. The mortgage company offered him a higher management position and an increase in salary that he could not turn down. This put them on a tight schedule to get everything done and arrive back in time for him to start his new job.

All this would have fallen into line just fine except for one thing. After they got back Esther decided that she did not want to move to California, or anywhere for that matter - *Much Ado for Nothing* to paraphrase W. Shakespeare. They returned home as owners of an empty duplex they did not want. They decided to rent it out for a while until they could sell it. When it finally sold they were overjoyed. Being in the landlord business was not to their liking.

Part Three

Chapter Twenty-three

It was now 1982, the year Ken would be graduating from high school and preparing for college. Dennis was in his sophomore year of high school. Chet was settled into his new job and Mavis was doing well in hers. Things were settling down from the aborted move of Esther to California and life was again moving along at a steady pace. As things had gone in Chet's life in the past, a period of relative peace and stability seemed to always be followed by some form of upheaval or drastic change. This pattern was still operative.

It was in the latter part of the year that an envelope arrived addressed to Chester Lee from one who had, practically speaking, dropped out of his life. The letter was postmarked "Chicago IL" and it was from his cousin, Connie. Inside the envelope was another envelope to which she had attached a note that said simply, "This is your real brother." -- *What on earth does that mean?*

Chet opened the envelope and found a letter, written in Chinese, addressed to Yee Ping, Connie's Chinese name. He asked Mavis to see if she could translate any of it. Mavis began to translate it into English to the best of her ability. The writer was begging Connie to forward the letter to his little brother, Chin Yuen Yick, who he had been trying to locate for the past forty years or, at the very least, give him his brother's address so he could contact him. The letter pleaded with her, since she was a mother, to understand why they had so diligently and for so long tried to find him. -- *For forty years this person had been trying to find his little brother?* He thought. *He must believe Connie knows where he is. And she sends it to me with this note attached, "This is your real brother." My God! What should I make of this? She gives no explanation of any kind. She never was one to talk much, but when she did say something, it was always truthful. She never lied. I don't know what to think. I never have and I never will understand these people who are supposed to be my people. Why would she send such a thing to me? What does she expect me to do about it?*

Discussing the letter with Mavis, he asked, "What do you make of this? Could she be saying that this guy is my real brother?"

"Why don't you call Connie and ask her why she sent it and what it means." Mavis replied. "She is the only one who can tell you what you need to know."

"I'll think about it. You know how people will do anything to get into the U.S. and this might be something like that." Chet responded. "It's such a strange thing for her to do! We haven't spoken in years. Not since Victoria and Harry moved to San Francisco. Why would she send this to me now? I'll have to think about what I'm going to do."

Chet kept pondering the letter and what he would say to Connie. He could not get the poignancy of the letter out of his mind. *Imagine a person trying for forty years to find his brother. Does her note mean that I could be this brother? Could this lead to finding my real parents? No, that's too far-fetched - but wouldn't it be fantastic if it were true! No, this has to be the scheme of some Chinese to make a connection to get into the U.S. It's got to be something like that. Most Chinese would love to find a rich relative in the U.S. so they could come here. All our friends from Taiwan and Hong Kong have warned us about how many Chinese want to come here.*

Ken and Dennis were intrigued about the letter, too. Who knows? They might find a long lost family they never knew they had. The boys knew little of all the negative emotional baggage that was making their dad hesitant, though deep in his heart he yearned for it to be true. They were all skeptical, but hopeful that it might be true.

Chet decided the only thing to do was to call Connie and ask what all this meant. He called the next day, she answered and they had a long talk. She told how she came to send him the letter.

Connie had two sons, one who was especially close to her had just passed away after a long illness. She was very vulnerable because of this. The letter she sent to Chet was originally mailed to her at an apartment address she had moved from over two years before. The mailman was persistent but about to give up trying to deliver it because he had no forwarding address. One day he happened to speak to another tenant who said she knew Connie's new address. She gave him the address and he forwarded the letter.

Connie told Chet, "When I received the letter and read it, I decided it was time to give it to you. All the other relatives, and I, had been so afraid of Victoria all those years that we never acknowledged even the slightest hint of your past and ignored all the letters. Having just lost my son, I felt this secrecy had gone on long enough. Chin Yuen Xu, who wrote the letter, is your older brother. He now lives in Indonesia. He has been writing letters to every relative and friend he knew in the U. S. throughout all these years trying to find you. In fear of Victoria's orders, no one ever answered him or passed on any of his letters. I'm tired of this and decided that you have a right to know, so I sent you his letter. I assure you he is your blood brother, your real family."

Chet was completely overwhelmed and speechless at the prospect of this. Connie urged him to get in touch with his brother to see what came of it. She said to him over and over, "He *is* your real brother, your biological brother."

Chet could not overcome being skeptical. Connie was a good Christian and would not make up something like this or lie to him about such a critical matter, but this was an amazing revelation and it took time to come to terms with such news. If it were true, how would he answer the letter anyway? He couldn't write Chinese and could only speak a meager amount of phrases in the language. Were he to write to this person, it would have to be done correctly and he wasn't sure Mavis could do it well enough. This meant he would have to find a translator. That way he could write in English exactly what he wanted to say, then have a good translator put it into proper Chinese so there would be no misunderstandings. It would take time, but if this poor fellow has been trying for forty years to locate his brother, a little more time shouldn't matter that much. No need to rush into anything.

The entire family was in awe not only at how the letter happened to reach Connie but the fact that after all these years she would finally decide to reveal this monumental secret! They talked about all the letters this man had written for all those years getting no response from anyone, yet he persevered. This last letter would also have been lost if that mailman had not happened to speak to the one person in that complex that knew Connie and her new address. It's quite a miraculous chain of events.

For the next several weeks Chet could not get this latest revelation out of his mind and the impact it would have on his life, were it true. He had finally freed himself of his confusion with the Chinese culture and the dark cloud that Victoria created, although it still hovered in the corners of his mind. Did he want to chance revisiting any of this? His life right now was fruitful, satisfying, and peaceful. He was very happy being away from all those unfathomable dictums, taboos, and fears. He would indeed, have to give this some long, hard, serious thought.

Chapter Twenty-four

Getting in touch with this person Connie claimed was his real brother did not prove as easy as one might think. With Chet's skepticism still a strong factor, urgency was not the main player in this scenario. Curiosity does not necessarily breed urgency. He did want to find out the truth, but with so many disappointments and frustrations in his past he was not eager to lay himself open to more of the same. Between finding translators, mailing addresses that were misdirected, misspelled, and/or missent it was a couple years before they communicated directly.

Chet did write to him a few weeks after receiving his letter, but for some unknown reason his "real brother" never got it. After waiting several months for a reply and not receiving one, Chet decided to try again. In this time period there were several unsuccessful attempts made. Even with Connie's help no reply was forthcoming.

Some excerpts from the letters Chet wrote were as follows:

"...I received your letter via Yee Ping...and wasn't sure how to respond properly. I am very happy to hear from you, although I was very surprised. In 1982 I was told by Yee Ping that you had tried to contact me. At that time I tried to reach you by way of Yee Ping, but was unsuccessful. ...

I have felt that something was missing in my life and then to find out that I have a real family somewhere in China... I do look forward to meeting you, hopefully soon...

My name is Lee Gock Keung. I was brought to Chicago in July of 1947 ... I do not know anything about my real parents, as my adopted parents never told me about my background. I could not get any information from any of my relatives, even after my adopted parents passed away in 1967. I did not have any brothers or sisters while living with my adopted parents, whose English names were Harry and Victoria Chin. My English name is Chester, although everybody calls me Chet. I was supposed to be adopted by a family with the last name of Lee, and that is how my English name is Chester Lee. Perhaps you can tell me what my true date of birth is. I was told it is May 14, 1941.

Please write to me, and give me more information about yourself and the rest of my family. I understand that I am the second oldest... Please excuse the fact that I do not write Chinese anymore... I would appreciate it if you can give me more information, dates of birth, names of all my family members, including yourself. Questions such as marriages, children from those marriages, birth-dates, etc.

As the several letters written by both seemed to be like ships passing in the night, persistence on both their parts paid off. Chet's last letter (excerpts printed above) was dated May 25, 1985. Then, finally, he received that first direct reply. The following excerpts from the letter to Chet (translated version) from Chin Yuen Xu, his "real brother", was dated May 17, 1985:

We haven't seen each other for so many years. I've been looking for you all this time, but I couldn't find you. Our father was asking for you on his deathbed...We asked around for your address for a very long time...When I received the letter, I was so happy I cried... Since we left home until now, you were very young then and now we are so old. To think about it is very sad, but what can we do?

Do you remember the past? I doubt it. Since 1948 I have been in Indonesia for 37 years. When our parents were alive, I sometimes mail some money to them, but these past years I have had bad luck in business and I have 14 children. My expenses are huge and my income is so little, so you understand my situation... I have a total of 11 sons and 3 daughters. I got married at 22 and am now 56 years old...

After you left home, we had one more brother and sister. Your brother's name is Ren Kan and sister's name is Shin Yee. They all have their own family. Ren was born in 1948 and Shin was born four years later. It's pitiful that we have never met each other... Please mail me a picture of your family. Don't forget that we are brothers. We will talk again.

As previous mistakes in addresses were corrected and the letters that were not lost caught up with each other, doubt about Chin Yuen Xu being his "real brother" was dispelled when Chet received a picture of him. His brother looked exactly like him! Ken and Dennis both said, "That's exactly how you will look in twelve years when you're his age, Dad!" What would later become evident as a family characteristic, the right eye being slightly smaller than the left, showed clearly in the picture. Mavis and the boys reaffirmed, "He's got to be your brother!" This picture was the final litmus test for Chet. He knew now that he had found his real family. All doubt completely disappeared.

Letters began to pour back and forth between him and his older brother as well as between him and his younger brother and sister. None of them knew English and he knew little or no Chinese. He needed a good translator which could be a bit of a problem, but that mattered little. It was worth anything knowing that he had found his real family!

Letters back and forth now began with – *Dear Big Brother - To My Second to Oldest Brother - Dear Youngest Sister - To Younger Brother - Dear Brother and Sister-in-law - Dear Sister, Brother-in-law, Nieces and Nephews* and so forth.

Chet asked that with all the letters he wanted to write to them - his new-found siblings - would they mind if he wrote one letter, had it translated into Chinese, then sent copies to each of them. He had found a couple good translators and did not want to overburden them with translating so many letters. These translators gave him good advice on Chinese protocol and customs and advised him on how to respond properly. Chet wanted to fill them all in on the same information and had the same questions for all of them for the most part. The letters began to sail back and forth across the Pacific revealing more and more details about their lives in the past and how they were getting along now. There was so much they had to catch up on about each other and as their relationship grew there would have to be plans made to meet sometime in the future.

Letters from all three of his new-found family members were packed with information from how tall they were and how much they weighed to what they ate and how they spent their days. Of course, they wanted to know all these same things about Chet's life.

Many beautiful Chinese phrases in the letters were not always captured in the translation. For instance, the greeting *To second oldest brother* was actually expressed in Chinese as *To one from the same womb*. The concept of how his mother was always thinking of him and how, at the same time, he was sensing something missing in his life - *You were drifting like a cloud - asking where are my people and country*; now, *as falling leaves drop to the roots we have found you and you have found us*. How wonderfully

146

poetic and sensitive compared to the business-like way they are expressed in English! [1]

Chet replied in August of 1985:

Dear Youngest Brother and Sister (and oldest Brother),
I was so happy when I received both your letters yesterday...Older brother had told me he was going to write you both and let you know that he had received my letters. You cannot believe how happy I am...Thank you for the picture of you both and my parents. Your letters are very warm and you make me feel a part of the family, even though we have never met each other.

While we can talk about the past in order to get to know each other better, we should not dwell on the sufferings of the past, as we can do nothing about it, but rather, look forward to the future. I honestly do not know when we can afford to go to China to visit you, but we will try as soon as possible...

I promise to send some snapshots. Please send pictures of you and your families, as well as Mom and Dad, and myself when I was in China. I do not have any pictures from China as my adopted parents kept them and did not give them to me, and now they are lost...

My wife's name is Mavis and her Chinese name is Mei Yee. She speaks Cantonese and was born in Hong Kong. We have two boys, Kenneth, the oldest, whose Chinese name is Houng Doc and Dennis, the youngest, whose Chinese name is Houng Yen...

I want to know more about you and your family and how you live. If I ask questions that seem stupid or insulting to you, please forgive me, as it is out of ignorance, not disrespect...

I am enclosing some stickers with my address on them. Use

---

[1] - Phrases like these, when notated by the translators, are enclosed in brackets [ ] in the letters from China quoted in the following chapters.

these on the envelope when you write to me and the letters will be delivered more easily.

With love to you and your families,
Chet

After being an 'only child' in a loveless family all of his remembered life, his immediate family count at this beginning point in their reunion was:

Brothers -- 2
Sisters -- 3 (2 deceased)
Mother and father -- both deceased
Nieces and nephews -- 18.

That was quite a leap in the number of relationships with people who really love you (outside of his wife and children) and have no inhibitions in expressing it - zero to twenty-one.

The excitement of each letter, getting acquainted with all these people who had been looking for him all these years, discovering his real roots, finding out about all that had happened and why it happened, was, for Chet, filling in that last big hole in his life, the mystery of who he really was.

Chapter Twenty-five

W ith all these new-found family members, their Chinese names were getting to be a little confusing. Each translator would have a different interpretation and spelling of the names based on that translator's background and dialect. To keep straight on who's who, Chet decided to give American names to all his new siblings and their families. These were usually related to the meanings of their Chinese names or simply a phonetic association. Oldest brother, however, became known as Charlie. With their family name Chin sometimes translated as Chan, that could make him Charlie Chan like that dogged detective who never gave up in solving a mystery. That was rather fitting for Charlie considering how diligent he had been in finding Chet. Youngest brother became known as Sam (Silent Sam) because he didn't write that much or as often. Although they didn't realize it at the time, Sam in Chinese means the number 3 and Sam is the third male in his family. Youngest sister became Gail (Gabby Gail) because she did write a lot and quite often. This made it much easier for Chet and his family to keep track. There was no disrespect meant in choosing these names. His brothers and sister seemed to like them too.

On 6/28/85 Charlie wrote:

...You say you wrote in 1981, but I did not get the letter. You wrote my address wrong.

Let me tell you about myself/yourself. Our father at the age of 12 got smallpox. Infection grew, his hands and legs were disabled. That's why our family was so poor. You had two sisters, Jade Leaf and Leaf of Moon. Both died at ages of 1-2 years. Our mom so superstitious – 'brother has heavy footsteps', meaning me – and she thinks it's because of me that they died. That's why you were sent away – afraid you would die also. I left when I was 12 years old. Father had 3 brothers still living in Indonesia. One brother was killed in the Japanese War.

There was a contract between your adopted mother and natural mother. The contract is still in China and it says, "Although we give you to your adopted mother, your natural parents are to be like god-parents so you would still know them. Our true relationships would be honored and we would have a chance to get you back." After you left China for Chicago your adopted parents sent $10.00 in U.S. money to your father, but they did not give a return address, so we couldn't reach you. Yee Ping's mother explained that Harry and Victoria were afraid that if they gave you money you would give it back to our family so they didn't ever write back to your natural parents. We couldn't reach you. We tried for tens of years. We felt very bitter about this. Your father, on his deathbed, said, "You must find him!" You know that your adopted mother and your natural mother were good childhood friends even sleeping over and your mother knows Vicky is of a good nature and that's why we chose her to be your adopted mother...

...Your birth date is correct. I only went to school for 1½ years... My Chinese is not good and I don't know English... Since 1948 in Indonesia I have done jewelry/goldsmith business.

150

A Pawn of Fate

I raise all these children so I don't have much money. I want to own my own business but I don't have enough money. Now that I write this letter I believe you understand the situation. My heart wants to do, but my ability can't...

I have never seen my other brother and sister, but we write to each other... I hope we can both go back to China and visit our parents' graves, but I don't have money for travel to China...

In July of 1985 a letter came from Gail (younger sister) in which she said:

Dear Brother and Sister-in-law:

I received the letter from oldest brother in Indonesia. After we haven't heard anything from you in over 30 years we finally heard from you! I'm so happy. We miss you very much. I would have written sooner but I was waiting for the pictures of myself, my brother and our parents.

...Father passed away 9 years ago at age 76. Mother passed away 14 years ago at age 61. She had nine children. I have four older sisters, one stillborn brother [who did not eat mother's rice], now only left three brothers. Because of the circumstances...I and younger brother stayed at home. Things were very bad. If parents didn't let you go to America maybe you won't have survived today. All these things left parents heart-broken.

My brother here is 38 and I am 34. I work in the village farming. I was married in 1975 and my husband, age 35, is in construction...we have 2 daughters ages 7 and 9 in grade school. My home is 10 miles from my brother at our parents' village.

Brother, I want to understand you some more. What do you do, how many children do you have and how old are they? I hope you can send some more letters and keep us tied together. I don't have much schooling, so not good writing. Please excuse me...Hope you get everything you want.

Best regards,
Your sister

151

Also, in July of 1985 a letter came from Sam (younger brother). He wrote:

...I don't know why we have to suffer all this separation. You don't know Chinese and I don't know English, so I can't describe family history very well...

You say you weigh 165 lbs. and are 6' tall. I am 5' tall and weigh 130 lbs. Are you like-Chinese (complexion, skin)? Since I was 9 years I help parents with household. At 14, I stopped going to school and helped with farm work, so I don't know many things. When I learned from your letter that you have 2 boys going to university I am very happy about that.

I remember our dad on his deathbed asking for you repeatedly and asked us to try to find you. It is regretful...In 1948 when Japan invaded China, everybody is so poor, people scattered, father couldn't work or walk and mom had to get rice 'shells' (*used for pig food or fertilizer*) to feed us. Older brother worked, but almost starved to death. Yee Ping's mother suggested you get out of China and got papers to get you out. Mom always said you were very clever and smart. On the eve of your departure you told dad that you would never forget him and their names. You gave mom a chess piece from your pocket and said, "This is for you to remember me by." She always held it and kept it...

Dad received your envelope and $10, but no address...no word until now, nor could we get any information...We were able to contact Yee Ping's mother...but no response...big brother wouldn't give up...Dad died with eyes opened. We never thought that we would be able to contact you. Now we are so happy we couldn't sleep for a few days.

I read Father's diary and it has your birth date on it. It's April 10, 1941.[2] Eat your birthday cake on April 10! We still have your picture before you left. Do you have your own copy? Your sister and I sent our family picture...please mail us your

---

[2] This date was according to the Chinese calendar.

family picture.

Wish you the best. I have a lot to say…some other day.

Letters and pictures came in a continual flow, each revealing amazing facts and sentiments. The excitement of finding each other; questions about what the family did to survive with his father's poor health; further proof of family resemblances were so wonderful to hear. Charlie wrote that their sister looks just like their mom. He also said that he, Charlie, has "hair just like yours – our father doesn't have hair also!"

Sam wrote: "You look so much like older brother – same mold. Your mouth looks like father's and eyes like mother's. Shape of your body looks like mother. Your hair looks like father's – not too much of it. I'm also losing my hair. I thought that since you lived in America for so long you must look like an American, but you don't. I see youth in your pictures. You look alert and joyful. It's just how mom described you – very bright, but naughty."

The letters also included directions to get to their homes- "…take a plane to Hong Kong; a train to Canton (3-4 hours); then another train to Toi Shan (4 hours); from Toi Shan to our house is only 3 miles…" all this in the anticipation that they must one day meet and see each other.

There definitely was going to be a trip back to China. The question was when and how soon would they be able to save enough money for the transportation and all that Chet wanted to do for his new-found family. He would need to pay for their trips because they had no money. In his letters Chet asked what kind of clothes they wore; what was the height and weight of each adult and child; when was school out so the whole families could all be together; did they have gas or electricity in their houses; when was the weather best; and on and on. He needed to know about government and local regulations, not only for travel and visas, but for dress and customs. Things are so casual here in California that he did not want to offend anyone or break any rules. Being used to many creature comforts, they also wanted to be able to stay in a hotel while they were there. He wanted to have all the families experience this for the first time, too.

One critical consideration was about diet. Chet was not about to indulge in any of the considered delicacies there such as snake, dog, cat, rat and other species. He announced to them that he would be happy to pay for them to have these delicacies but he would absolutely not be joining them in this.

Sam responded: "Chet, why don't you like to eat snakes, rats and cats? We Cantonese love to eat that stuff and its very nutritious and beneficial to the body. What kind of utensils do you eat with? We use chopsticks. From TV we notice Americans use forks."

There were so many considerations to be addressed that it would take some time to plan the trip and especially, to save up enough money to do all the things they wanted to do and accomplish while they were there.

Unexpectedly, an opportunity to teach some computer classes in Peking was offered to Chet. This came about when he had dinner with a Chinese friend who lives here in the U.S. and a visiting professor from Peking. The professor said that China is very anxious to have the Chinese people more computer-savvy. This is important in their campaign to modernize the country and they seem to favor the idea of educated ex-patriots returning if only for a visit. Computers are totally unknown to the majority of their people and since computers are now at the root of everything that happens in today's world they need to offer classes to anyone who wants to learn. He asked if Chet would consider coming to Beijing to teach for five days, three hours per day. Chet liked the idea. This would not be a paid position, but that was not important to him. He regarded it as an opportunity to make a contribution to the country where he was born and it helped establish a time to schedule the reunion trip. There would be a translator for teaching the class, but Chet wanted to learn Mandarin to be a more effective teacher. Although his family speaks Cantonese the languages are related closely enough that it would help prepare him to learn Cantonese. As time for the reunion drew closer, however, it became clear that going to Beijing to teach for five days was not going to be possible for logistical reasons. This would have to wait until a later time, another trip.

The excitement of actually meeting face-to-face was gathering uncontrollable momentum and excitement. They all wrote to Chet, "We are going to kill a chicken! We will have 3 fresh-meat dishes to honor the gods, pay respect to ancestors and parents so that parents will know that we have found our blood brother. We will invite the village elders to a feast of killed chickens to give thanks to our parents that their spirit looks over us because of your goodness; you are pleasing your parents and we will have a reunion. If it weren't for our reunion in this lifetime we would not have been able to have a roasted pig to offer our ancestors."

Charlie added: "Our family is the only one that has not gone back to the village…uncles will be so happy. [It's like a thunderclap that rings throughout the sky]."

The trip was tentatively scheduled for some time in the Fall of 1986.

Chapter Twenty-six

As Chet learned more about his family and how they lived, he began sending money in each letter. Realizing how these conditions of poverty had kept Charlie, Sam and Gail from getting an education, he was very concerned that this not be the fate of his nieces and nephews. He sent money for their books and school fees. He strongly urged them to do well in school and to learn English. He suggested that they might want to consider studying in the U.S. in later years. He offered his help and support in any way possible.

From Charlie's letters, Chet learned of the intricacies and entanglements in sending money to Indonesia:

"...I received your letter, pictures, and my birthday present of $100.00 U.S. dollars. I was so happy that I cried because all these years I never received a birthday gift from anyone besides my children. I'm sorry about the money order. I can't cash it. I had to ask a friend who has an account with an American bank to deposit it in his account and then give me the cash...You wrote my name wrong on the check, please write it correctly next time."

Evidently, officially or unofficially, the Indonesian government regards and treats Chinese as aliens, even those born in Indonesia. Charlie had to buy an Indonesian name from the leader of his village in order to conduct business there. That was the name that must be on the check in order for it to be cashed. Anything a Chinese person wants to do there seems to involve a pay-off to someone.

For Sam and Gail in China, the best way to send money was to:

"...put cash in the envelope with the letter and use registered mail. This way we can avoid post office investigation. If you send cash the exchange rate for $100 U.S. dollars is 400 People's Republic of China dollars. If you send a check then you only get 290 PRC dollars."

With his lessons in Chinese, Chet was now beginning to write short phrases and greetings in Chinese to his brothers and sister. This pleased his siblings very much and they complimented him on his efforts. The major part of all letters was still done by the translators, of course.

In a later letter, Charlie expressed concern for Chet and whether their needs and ways of doing things might be a burden to him:

"Chet, I am not trying to be funny or unappreciative, but has our correspondence (with Gail and Sam, also) caused you problems or headaches or cost you money? You sent money to Sam and Gail for New Year because in China, when you have some money for the New Year it's as joyful as a shooting star from heaven.

"Are you a Christian? I took time to write this letter and make it clear for you to read. Okay, I wish that your children study hard and make a name for themselves in the world. In Indonesia it doesn't matter if you are smart or not. Once you graduate from high school you can't go further. College costs hundreds of dollars. That's why all my children upon graduation from high school start working at a job.

"How soon can you start reading my letters in Chinese? You have made such progress. You are so smart that in such a short time you have shown so much progress. It is very admirable."

Chet asked them if they had appliances like a refrigerator, washer, dryer, or TV. Gail replied that they did not have a TV, but the children went to other houses to watch it. She believes that they learn a lot from these shows and said, "Chinese TV has many educational programs and English sessions. " She said that no one in the village has a refrigerator. She described the house they live in, which is borrowed from her father-in-law's uncle: it has one bedroom, one kitchen, living room and is also used by another family. They have 1.5 acres of land on which to plant rice, but the land is owned by the government and a percentage of their crop must be given to the state.

Sam talks about his house (which is their ancestral home) in this way: "...The house we are living in now was built by money sent by #4 Uncle (our father's oldest brother) to #1 Uncle. #4 Uncle gave us one unit to live in. Our father is #3 son. Grandfather did not leave a house to our father. In 1940 the house was finished – it's as old as you. According to mother, you were born in this house...The government gives me a little over 2 acres of land to cultivate. Every year we must give 1/3 of our crops to the government. What's left is for us and is barely enough. I have to go to market to make up the difference. The government boasts about what the farmers have accomplished. Actually only a few have become rich. Most are still living in poverty...

"You ask if we have TV or refrigerator. Those two items are very expensive...for farmers who cultivate the land, those two items are an impossible dream. It costs at least $1500.00 to buy a 14" TV."

Gail wrote:

"...We live in the countryside. Everything is far behind in living conditions. We have had electricity since 1963...but we still do not have a water system. We have to get water from a well and bring it to the house on our shoulders in buckets. In Toi Shan part of the population has gas. In our village we cannot afford coal, let alone gas. We go outside to gather firewood or grass and dry it in the sunlight to use for cooking and heat...Now the weather is cool and comfortable, about 77° F. with the hottest temperature at about 95°. The coldest it gets is about 35° to 38°. Winter is better than summer."

A very important thing Chet began asking each of them in his letters was for them to consider whether they would like to come to live in the U.S. This would be a very involved process that should be started as soon as possible because, at best, it would take several years for all the paperwork to be approved. He explained all the problems and restrictions that go along with setting this up. He is only able to bring the immediate family member first, and then they, after living here for a year, can apply to bring the rest of their family over. It would require a year of separation from the family. Charlie responded:

"You asked me if I wanted to go to America. I really want to go, but there's a fortune teller that told me I won't live past 60 years of age, so it'll only be for a few years. It doesn't make much sense for me to go. My life expectancy seems short, like mother's. Well, fortune teller is one story. I'd just let it be. God will decide it."

Gail's response was:

"Many thanks for you applying for us to come over. It is very thoughtful of you and with your ability to do this, it makes our whole family very happy. Your idea of having me going first and then the rest of the family coming over later -- I understand your reasoning and the difficulties. In your letter you mention the hardships and it is very practical and reasonable...No matter what happens, it will be much better to go to the U.S. than to stay in China. My husband is also a hard worker and intelligent...His education is above average..."

Sam's response was:

"Chet, regarding the matter of my emigrating to the U.S., I went to the courts and inquired and it is possible to start the application...I have a few items to clarify before I can proceed with the documents...We will have to wait. No matter how hard the work, I am willing to do the work. If you have a good plan, we'll go with it...I'm determined to go to U.S., be thrifty and work hard. Our entire family being able to go to U.S. is very fortunate. Hopefully in 2-3 years I can repay you the money. I do not want to cause you any hardship because of us."

After further investigation, Chet wrote back:

"I must apologize. In my last letter about immigration laws, I told you some wrong information...the correct information is:...I can only apply for immediate family to come over. With fifth preference, (*fifth preference refers to the priorities for immigration – 1st is spouse, 2nd child, 3rd parent, 4th fiancée, and 5th sibling*) your whole family can come over at once, but it will take 5-6 years for that quota to come up. That is a long time to wait, but your family will not be separated. The disadvantages...the costs of your entire family coming over will be all at one time...around $2000 U.S... There are a few other options and many possible complications, but all involve a long wait. We need to get to work on all the documentation required and then decide the best way to proceed."

It was a problem for Gail and Sam to prove that they

are brother and sister to Chet with Chet's confusion in names. Their legal family name is Chin. His is Lee. Also, the confusion about Chet's birth date: Chinese calendar – April 10th, family records – May 28th, or birth date of the Lee's dead son whose identity he assumed in order to get into the U.S. – May 14th. These were all things that could be worked out but not without some difficulty and delays. Sam wrote:

"…Regarding emigration I am already working on it…On your application you did not include your adoptive parents, such as names and birth dates, and when they passed away. At the same time you have to make a photocopy of your passport showing your name and birth date on it.

"Also, along with this letter, I enclosed the letter of your "Sale" for you to copy and send photocopy back to me. The courts require this document to prove that we are brothers. At home it is difficult to make copies, and this document is several decades old. It is very fragile, so take good care of it. When mother was still alive I tried to keep it out of her sight. One time she happened to see it and immediately she fainted…but she asked me to safe-keep it. That's why I have it to this date; hope you don't mind."

Chet emphasized over and over in his letters the necessity for all the family to learn English if they were going to live in America.

Gail wrote: "…We will figure out how to find time to learn English and also we are older and not educated even in Chinese, so it'll be harder to learn, but we are determined to slowly learn it. Just like you said, 'Do our best, learn as much as we can, that's all we can do.' We must listen to your words so we won't disappoint you."

Sam replied: "Chet, I only have grade school education, my grammar is very poor. It would be very difficult for me to learn English...[like an elephant learning bird language]. I'm determined to learn English as much as I can and when I get to the U.S., I'll learn more."

Chet now realized that insisting that Sam and Gail learn English was asking too much of someone with a very limited education in their own language. A future based on English was going to be more the responsibility of their children. He would shift his urging to learn English more toward the children and encourage his brothers and sister to learn as much English as they reasonably can.

There was much to be done to prepare for them to be housed and employed when they all arrive. They could live with Chet and Mavis until they got a feel for living here, but would soon need a place of their own.

Charlie was focused on the trip back to the village in China and their reunion. It did not seem that coming to the U.S. was in the books for him at his age. He was extremely excited about the prospect of going back to the village and couldn't stop talking and writing about it. He told Chet there was an elderly relative still living in the village who knew all about what happened with him when he left the village and China for a new life in America. "There's a lot that hasn't been said. It's too much to cover in a letter. When I see you, then I'll explain everything to you," Charlie wrote.

Chapter Twenty-seven

*P*lans for the reunion were full speed ahead on both sides of the Pacific as was the preparation and filing of their emigration papers. The reunion would be happening soon, but emigration for the families would be many years from now. Once all the documentation for emigration was accepted in both China and the U.S., it would be a long wait until the processing was finished and their names came up in the order of the quota for each year. Chet had the itinerary for the reunion trip pretty well set from his side and his family was arranging the reunion celebration on their side of the Pacific.

A fellow student in Chet's Mandarin class was also from the Toi Shan area. She advised Chet to work with a travel agent she knew who was very familiar with that area of China. She advised him that the most economical way to see more of the country and meet all the requirements for the trip was to connect with a tour group in China. Dennis decided not to go along on the trip because the time off from school would necessitate delaying his graduation from college, so it would be just Chet, Mavis and Ken flying into Hong Kong for the first leg of the trip. They would arrive on October 6th and visit for a few days with Mavis's father who was now quite elderly. They would meet Charlie there on October 12th and proceed to Toi Shan by boat for the reunion. They would connect with the tour group in Canton on October 17th after their five-day visit to the village.

Susan, Charlie's oldest daughter, is married and lives in Hong Kong. She speaks a little English and is very knowledgeable about making connections and getting around the area so, besides just meeting her as a family member, she would be invaluable in helping them communicate. Her husband, Fan, teaches at a Hong Kong college and she works full-time. Their names, Susan and Fan, were already established so there was no need to make up new ones. Neither Susan nor her husband would be able to go to the reunion, but she would visit the village later whenever possible. They would meet Charlie and make arrangements for him to connect with Mavis, Chet and Ken.

For Charlie to leave Indonesia seemed to be an extremely complicated and expensive process. He had not left the country since he arrived almost 40 years ago. He would have to have a passport, visa, ID card, and a sponsor. If he owed any taxes, including the foreigner's tax, these had to be paid in full before he would be given his documents and allowed to leave the country. Of course, there were all those bribes to be paid along the way, too. It finally worked out that if he used a travel agency it could be his sponsor, thus eliminating one big problem. Of greatest concern was whether all the documentation could be completed and issued in time for the reunion that was now only five months away.

Charlie did not give much information about his immediate family. He still had seven children in school – three in first grade, two in second grade and one each in middle school and high school. Having so many children must have been a factor in his choosing not to come to the U.S. In his letters he spoke of them with pride and talked about how hard they study and work. That's a lot of people to talk about and describe in a letter. He said he would tell Chet all about them when they met at the reunion.

It was so important that they all be there. Gail and Sam had never seen Charlie nor had he seen them. They had only communicated by letter. Through all these years they, of course, knew of Chet only as a long-lost brother they had – somewhere. When Chet and Charlie last saw each other, Chet was five years old and Charlie was sixteen. Charlie was now 56 and after such a hard life, his health and strength were on the wane. He said this was probably the only opportunity he would ever have to go back to the village. There is so much to catch up on – almost 40 years worth! All those loose ends they had been trying so hard to grasp were now beginning to weave together into a colorful tapestry of discovery and life.

To return to his birthplace, where he'd spent the first five years of his life, was of monumental importance to Chet. Vague recollections were deep in his mind. When they might surface he was never sure of their source or if they were real memories at all. Many of them were starting to make sense now. How sad that this could not have come to fruition while his parents were alive. As he was growing up in Chicago, everyone around him in the family knew all this and never gave him an inkling of it. It is part of the Chinese culture that when you are adopted your former life no longer exists. They certainly held tight to that belief. *Well,* he thought, *at least now it is happening, even after such an incredibly long time. Dwelling on how easily this could have happened years before cannot change anything and serves no useful purpose now.*

Sam expressed the feelings of all the family members in

a letter dated two weeks before the reunion:

"… we are going to be reunited soon, and I'm so happy I couldn't sleep last night thinking about this. Just thinking back, our parents had hopes of seeing you again and now, we have got this opportunity of being together. Sometimes tears roll down my cheeks. So very gratified that you and your family are going to visit our parents' gravesite and they will be at peace knowing we are all reunited."

Chet gave Sam's wife the name Charlene after seeing her picture and being told the meaning of her Chinese name. Her Chinese name means – of beautiful or delicate appearance. Sam is a policeman in the village. Chet called their oldest child Roy, as his name means - fast champion (maybe a throwback to Chet's fascination as a child with cowboys Roy Rogers and Gene Autry and Autry's horse, Champion?). Their daughter he called Wendy because her name means – clever still. Roy is in junior high school and Wendy is in fourth grade. Charlene did the farming for the family. She had to get water from the well for the family and the fields. She worked very hard from dawn to dusk planting, taking care of and harvesting the rice and vegetables she grew for the family – and for the government. She also had to take care of their children. When the children were older, they helped out.

Gail's husband became known as John. His Chinese name means – fourth original. Gail and John have two daughters. Their names became Misty and Melody. Misty's Chinese name means – wonderful sunset, and Melody's – wonderful piano or harp. Both girls are in elementary school. John is a construction foreman. When he was offered a better job with a company in Toi Shan they moved there from the village and were able to rent an apartment owned by the company he worked for. Gail does the farming of their land in the village because they cannot afford to lose it. She has to travel back and forth, a distance of about 7 miles, to tend their crops - mainly rice and peanuts - which became quite a logistical problem. She sells the rice and peanuts at a street stall in the city. Later she hopes to be able to find a job in the city.

Along with the excitement of reunion there was also some trepidation about how they would be able to communicate, how to deal with the vast cultural differences, different personalities and expectations, etc. As Charlie said in one of his letters, "It's like a chicken talking to a duck." This will be quite a challenge in all these areas!

Chet had requested that the travel agency make arrangements for him and his family to stay in a modern hotel in Toi Shan. This hotel would have all the modern conveniences: TV, indoor plumbing, air-conditioning, heating, Western food and other necessities for *foreigners* from the West. They also made arrangements for transportation from the port to the hotel.

Chet was paying for the expenses of the reunion, both for travel and for the celebration itself. Charlie talked about inviting the whole village to celebrate with dinner at a restaurant. He wanted not only to share their joy at being reunited, but to show all the villagers that their family was no longer subject to derision. He had said in his letters that many villagers took advantage of their father's disabilities and looked down on the family. Chet wasn't concerned about that at this point in his life. He just wanted to enjoy his family and honor their parents. Charlie was the one who suffered most from the villagers' unkind attitude in those early years. Sam and Gail did not experience it to the same degree. It was agreed finally that the banquet – the killing of those chickens – would be limited to family. Chet knew that inviting the whole village to a restaurant would be very costly. They agreed that just the fact that he was there was statement enough. They would visit with others but their celebration would be a family one and would take place in the village.

Sam wanted to schedule time to take Chet to the nearby Warm Springs for a healthful bath. He said their father took him there and said how he had taken Chet there when he was little. How excited they were that Chet would be able to see where he was born and lived his early years, and to connect with their life in a concrete way.

Meanwhile, Chet and Mavis were shopping for candy, clothing and toys and whatever they thought the families might need or like. They were going to send boxes of things to the families right away and then bring the rest with them on the trip. Charlie mentioned in one of his letters that he played badminton and had been playing it for 30 years. Having gotten all their sizes and likes in clothing they bought T-shirts, sweat shirts, jeans, stuffed animals and other toys. Three months went by before the boxes were delivered. Chet and Mavis had given them up as lost, when finally, letters came saying how excited they were to receive everything. The clothes fit well and the children loved the stuffed animals and slept with them every night. Gail mentioned they especially loved the Mickey Mouse shirts because, "The children like to catch mice to play with."

Chet and Mavis wanted to do all they could to try to help them have a little easier life. They were busy finding out the best way to get some larger items, like TVs and motorcycles or motorbikes, to them. It seemed that the easiest and most economical way to do this would be to purchase them in Hong Kong and have them shipped from there. They would see about this when they arrived in Hong Kong on their way to the reunion. They knew that once they met and saw how they lived, there would be other needs they would be aware of and could help with. Having lived such a comfortable life in comparison to theirs, it was important to Chet to help his family improve their living conditions in any way he could.

Chapter Twenty-eight

When October 6, 1986 finally arrived, Chet, Mavis, and Ken were all packed and ready to head for the airport. All their bags were stuffed with clothes, toys and treats for everyone in Chet's family. It was such a long-awaited time for all. With English-Chinese dictionaries at the ready, they got their numerous bags checked and boarded their plane. They arrived in Hong Kong the next day to spend several days with Mavis's father, who was now over 80 years old.

They contacted Charlie's daughter, Susan, and her husband, Fan, and met up with them when Charlie arrived from Indonesia later in the week. The reunion with Charlie was going to be an emotional one. His unbelievable persistence was about to be rewarded. Reuniting Chet to his birth family was, to them, of no less importance than the amazing feat of the 'Golden Spike' being driven in to join the two sections of the U.S. transcontinental railroad. When the two brothers met, the family resemblance was so obvious, they were almost like mirror images, one a little more aged than the other. Although Chet actually had no childhood memories of Charlie, Charlie had enough detailed remembrances for both of them and could hardly wait to talk about them in spite of the language difficulties.

They left by boat from Hong Kong arriving early afternoon at the port in Three Cities. There the pre-arranged car was waiting to take them to their hotel in Toi Shan where Chet had also reserved a room for Charlie.

Lined up in front of the hotel were Sam and Gail with their families anxiously awaiting their arrival. Emotions were running high as they greeted each other. The language barrier fell by the wayside as long hugs, smiles and tears that wouldn't quit prevailed. What elation in seeing and physically being together! Now a complete family, so caring and thrilled to be together, even though they had never known each other. Chet's nieces and nephews were equally in awe at meeting their mysterious uncle from the U.S. who had been the subject of much intrigue they had heard of throughout their lives.

After Mavis, Chet and Ken were settled into their hotel rooms, the whole family went to Gail's house in Toi Shan for dinner. The house was only a few blocks away from the hotel but those blocks were confusing ones to navigate. They did find their way and gave out the gifts they had brought with them from the U.S. There was great excitement over all the cookies, clothing, toys, and other treats. The color TVs they purchased in Hong Kong for the families would be delivered soon. Few families had TVs, so it was very exciting to have one of their own. In anticipation, John had already built a cabinet for it.

The next days were spent sight-seeing in the area and shopping in Toi Shan. Gail mentioned that a pagoda they were to visit had been there since she was born, but she had never had time to go to it. It was agreed that the ancestral celebration would best be postponed until the third day. Time was required for the roast pig to be prepared and brought to the village from the city as well as for other food preparations. Emotions were teeming over the reality of being reunited when it had seemed for so many years that this would never happen. Going to the village of their birth and visiting the graves of their parents, together, would be an emotional day for everyone, so it was important to reserve some time to catch a deep breath before that. The long trip and the hot, muggy weather had sapped the energy level for Chet, Mavis, and Ken.

In Toi Shan they bought antennas, surge suppressors and other items needed to hook up the TVs whenever they arrived. Since electricity was turned on only at certain hours of the day having a surge suppressor was important. That extra day without commitments was to serve as a surge suppressor of sorts for them, too, allowing a little time to relax and get to know each other. As well as a language and cultural difference, there was an age difference to be understood among these siblings. Chet, now 47 years old, was eleven years younger than Charlie and had no real memories of living in the village at all. Sam and Gail were nineteen and twenty-three years younger than Charlie and their experiences of living in the village differed from his. Thus, this upcoming visit to the village was approached from a different perspective by each of them, though heartily grounded in love for their parents and gratitude for being together.

Charlie, who was now 56 years old, had lived there during a time that was filled with hopelessness. Everyone was faced with starvation in the village in the 1930s and 40s. They stole food from the pigs to survive. Two younger sisters had died of starvation and that brought about the wrenching decision to 'sell' Chet to the couple in the U.S. to give him a chance for a better life. After the arrangements were made, Charlie was the one who had to take

Chet to the ship, the last one to see him as he left for the U.S. He then had to endure seeing the agony his parents suffered over this, so distraught they could hardly function. Charlie took on the heavy responsibility of finding Chet when betrayed by their friends who had adopted him, and no one would help. He had heard and felt the derision the family had undergone from villagers because his father was disabled and couldn't work like the other men. He knew of his mother's superstition about him as a bad omen because two other children had died and he had lived. He was possessed with a vision that he must fulfill the past and set things right. He needed to show that he had done this and thus, prove his worth. His vision was one of restoring his and the family image. His vision was rooted in the past, in *what was*.

Sam and Gail, who were now 37 and 34 years of age respectively, had also lived a stark, extremely difficult existence in the village. Their lives, however, did not seem to be rooted in the same pall of hopelessness that Charlie had experienced. Their vision was leaning more toward *what could be*. They, too, as did Charlie, had to give up an education after the third grade to work hard, full-time in the fields and scrounge for every morsel of food they could find. But the government was changing then and farm life had slowly begun to improve.

As the Communist government grew in power all villagers were ordered to gather every night in the community center to listen to readings of Mao's writings. If there was any sign of reluctance or drowsiness all could be severely punished. No consideration was given for their having worked all day in the fields in hot, humid weather. They had to be ready to answer any questions visitors (from the government) might throw at them about what they were learning from the readings.

A Pawn of Fate

As a young adult, Sam had been selected by the new communist government to be the reader of Mao's thoughts and always helped the villagers learn what they needed to know in these difficult situations. Now in his role as a policeman, he continued to help others as much as he could. He held a place of honor among the villagers and as a policeman had the power to influence favors when needed from officials in surrounding areas. Gail was also a hard worker and with Sam's help did the farming and took care of their parents' needs until their deaths. The villagers saw the family in a different light now, but Charlie, never having been back since he left 37 years ago, was not aware of these changes.

Sam and his family still live in the ancestral home. This is the house where all of them were born and now, is the focal point of this incredible reunion. The restoration of the family circle, including those gone before, would take place at this site where it all began. Sam, Gail, and Gail's husband, John, spent long hours and much effort in coordinating arrangements for this celebration and visit to the ancestral home and the graves of their parents. Their father's plea on his deathbed "You must find him!" had been answered. Chet had been found through Charlie's incredible perseverance in writing letters to any and everyone who might know where he was. It was to be a very special event for the family and the small village of Wen Qian Yu Hui.

Chapter Twenty-nine

Charlie, Sam, and Gail were entirely focused on show-ing their parents that their lost son has been found. This was each parent's dying wish. Every step in the planning of the reunion celebration was rooted in ancestral rites and traditions. In Chinese culture almost as much at-tention is given to the dead as was given them in life. An-cestors are a strong influence on the family and a powerful presence in preserving the family bond through many gen-erations. On special days the ancestors are appeased with their favorite foods, money (ceremonial money), and treats at the gravesite as well as in the ancestral hall. It is be-lieved that they have the power to reward or punish, and must be honored at all times because the well-being of the living is at stake. If the ancestors are pleased with the sac-rifices and affairs of their descendants, they give support and rewards. If they are not pleased, it is believed that they could bring severe punishment and cause them to struggle through a harsh existence. Ancestors are regarded almost as the spiritual leaders of the family and are consulted on all matters of importance.

The day had arrived for the official reunion. It began

when Chet and his family were picked up at the hotel by the pre-arranged van for the ride to the village to meet the rest of the family. Sam introduced them to the villagers going from house to house to meet those who were not out working in the fields. It was regarded as a Coming-Home party for Chet. This had been a major topic of conversation in the village for over a year now. At each house they were offered tea and some treats. It would have been an insult to refuse the offer, so they had had many cups of tea and sweets by the time they arrived at the ancestral home.

Chet's remembered experience of a home was of a well-constructed, well-cared-for, spacious and comfortable house with a nice yard. It was quite a switch to see dirt floors, walls made of dried mud and dung, no indoor plumbing or water, the pig sty right outside the living room and chickens and ducks at the back of the house. The house was in need of major repairs, but there was no money for the extensive work it would require. This was a very different way of life.

During this time, with just the family there, he saw the loft where he was born. It was a very soul-stirring moment for Chet realizing that this was the very spot where he came into the world. On the wall next to the stairs leading up to the loft he saw, protected in a glass case, his original passport photo and the only photo that existed of his parents. There also were the photos he had sent to the family after they'd found each other. Through the years the humidity and areas where the rain had seeped in had caused the older pictures to be in poor condition.

Sam removed a book from a table drawer. Held inside its pages was a very old paper that was folded, extremely fragile, and slightly crumbling. He unfolded it very gently and presented it to Chet and said, "This is the original adoption agreement signed by our parents, and by your adopted parents, Harry and Victoria." Then he took from his pocket the wooden chess pawn (shown on the cover of this book) that Chet had given their mother "to remember him by" when he left this home for the last time at the age of four. It was then that Chet felt the missing arc in his circle of life fall into place. It was an emotional moment for Chet who is not one given to such responses. Tears filled his eyes and he could not speak.

He listened to Charlie, who was there when all this took place, now in person, telling about the family and the village when Chet was sold and about his long search to find him. Most of this information Charlie had written in his letters, but hearing him say it in Chinese, standing next to him here where it all happened so long ago, bordered on an otherworldly experience for Chet.

Soon it was time to go to their parents' graves, the procession included people carrying the tray with the roast pig, the ultimate symbol of sacrifice and celebration, that had been prepared ahead of time and brought from the city. Others carried many plates of food of all kinds, some rode bicycles, kids rode on a tractors, some walked and the guests of honor, Chet, Mavis and Ken, were driven as near as possible to the site. There was a short walk through prairie grass, weeds and trees to the graves. The ancestral markers were made of wood and had been laid in the ground. The markers were inscribed with each parent's name and date of their death. Each person paid respects individually. The food was shared at the gravesite first as a gesture of love and respect for the ancestors and, especially, to reunite Chet with his parents in this celebration.

After the ceremony everyone returned to the village with the remainder of the food to celebrate, eat, talk, and get better acquainted. The villagers brought more food to the ancestral house. Drinks were limited to tea or water.

The villagers thought Ken and Chet were very tall. They enjoyed joking with Chet about his limited knowledge of Chinese customs and language although he was born there.

Gail was solicitous about the food and utensils for her American family. She was concerned that they might get sick not being used to some types of food being served and the methods of preparation. She made sure all utensils were rinsed with hot water. The villagers took the extra food home with them when the meal was over. Chet never figured out how they kept it for later when no refrigeration was available. He decided maybe it was just as well he didn't know.

Sam had gotten paper money in all denominations before the celebration and put the money into red envelopes as "lucky money." After the dinner he gave an envelope to every villager who attended. Those who had brought extra food or helped out in other ways such as driving the tractor or hauling food to the gravesite, received a little extra.

After this warm and welcoming experience, the next day was the day of departure for the American wing of the family. Charlie would stay on for another week at Gail's house. Sam had many commitments to meet since he also served as a judge for the area, so it was back to work for him.

As it turned out, Gail was the one who was sick the next morning. This was due to her staying up all night because she was so sad that the reunion was over. Chet did not expect her to be there to see them off, but she was there, crying quietly the whole time. They didn't know when they would see each other again. Chet and Mavis definitely intended to return but had no idea how soon, so no time frame was mentioned. They didn't want to make promises they might not be able to keep.

Chet, Mavis and Ken had to leave that morning to join

the tour group they had contracted with. Any deviation from their scheduled itinerary could be expensive. They traveled to Canton by bus, a 5-6 hour trip, and spent three weeks sight-seeing with the tour group before flying back to the U.S. They became friends with a somewhat older couple in the group who also lived in the Los Angeles area. The couple was going to Toi Shan, where the husband was born, following the tour and offered to pick up the TV set to take to Sam. They met Sam, Gail and their families, took them all to dinner and bought things for the children. The friendship has continued to this day.

Arriving home on November 9th, they were exhausted physically and emotionally, especially Chet. It was an amazing adventure and it would be some time before the effect of the trip would subside. For now, it would return to letters sailing back and forth across the Pacific until future plans could be defined.

Chapter Thirty

After a couple days of rest and adjusting to the time change, Chet, Mavis and Ken reconnected with daily life: returning to work, taking care of household chores, paying bills, working in the yard, and all other things requiring their attention. Letters were already on their way from China and Chet had soon written them a long letter about what the reunion had meant to him. It was as though they all had been given new life. Windows that had been sealed tight for so long were now opened wide and a wonderful fresh breeze was invigorating them all.

Letters from all the families, brothers and sister were filled with profuse gratitude and concern about all the money Chet had spent to make the reunion possible. They wrote of their love for Mavis and how lucky Chet was to have her. They said how much their parents had "...loved to eat roast pork...they could never have been able to afford it for them, but you provided it."

The children were all saying, "# 2 uncle and family loves us a lot and we love him, too!"

Sam also wrote, "...the short time you were here, the villagers, especially the elders, ...knew how you were when you were young. They all said you have good character, just like Father.

...they were afraid to shake hands, worried that you wouldn't like it...Ever since you went back there hasn't been a day gone by that somebody didn't come by and express how happy they were for me. That makes me so proud."

They asked many questions about how Chet felt personally after the trip. "How did you feel about the trip back to the village and China?" "Did you enjoy your trip?" "What was most interesting to you?" "...you were able to drink the village water, see the room you were born in, and appreciate the surroundings – flowers, grass, trees."

Chet, as one who is not known for being expressive of his feelings, wrote back, "We were very touched on how the entire village came out to the feast, bringing food and chickens, and spending all that time cooking. It's something I will always remember as long as I live and I appreciate them welcoming me so warmly...I was very emotional during the ancestral walk...You were so hospitable...it was one of the best times I have ever had. Our cultures are so different, yet you judged us only for what we are...I wish I had planned to spend more time with you. We enjoyed our trip to China very much. Most enjoyable was our reunion in Toi Shan, having my two brothers and my sister together, visiting our parents' gravesites, and just getting to know all of you better. This was definitely the best item on our trip, and we all agreed on this."

The next project to be dealt with was one Chet had discussed with all his family before he left. It was about obtaining a marker and improving their parents' gravesite. Sam and Gail wanted to take on the responsibility of seeing that done. Sam sold a few piglets to help pay for it and hired a "Wind Water" expert (similar to Feng Shui) who gives advice about everything required to accomplish this properly. He assured them that the graves were "in an excellent spot" (no need for them to be moved or disturbed) and the only problem was that the site was too small, "…to widen it would be even better and we will be more prosperous," Sam wrote. The main focus was to arrive at a plan for widening it, the shape of the finished site and the timing for doing it, and what materials, cement or marble, could be used as markers. Each of these things must be given very serious consideration. Accomplishing this will bring great honor to the ancestors and to the family.

Other letters focused on the future plans for Gail and Sam and their families coming to live in the U.S. – how to prepare and what to expect. Although this couldn't happen for a number of years Sam and Gail wanted to make sure that everything was in legal order for this huge event. Chet was most concerned that things go as smoothly as possible for them. The children were learning English, but, for the adults, as much as they wanted to, it was just too difficult to accomplish while keeping up with daily life. Chet provided them with Chinese-English dictionaries to gain some understanding of the language. He also sent many photographs of his neighborhood: stores (including items for sale with the price tags), streets, traffic, schools, scenery, food, grocery stores and insides of houses so they could see the kitchens, bathrooms, etc. as this would all be very new to them.

Chet made trips to China again in 1987, 1989, 1990, 1992, 1993, and for the last time in 1996. Mavis went with him as often as possible. On these trips back to the village they included some side trips, also. Mavis's father died in 1989 and they (Dennis and Mavis came with him on this trip) had visited him shortly before his death. On the 1993 trip, they went to Indonesia to visit Charlie and some of his family.

On that first trip back in 1987, Chet made a special effort to take Gail and Sam and their families to stay for several days in a large hotel in Guangzhou to experience modern things. They had never been out of the village or to any large metropolitan area. Chet was thrilled to see them delighting in ice cold drinks, hot coffee, chocolate chip cookies, hamburgers, ice cream, and chocolate candy for the first time. Seeing big buildings, elevators, traffic moving at high speed, department stores, amusement parks and going on all the amusement park rides had them wide-eyed and amazed.

Sam's wife, Charlene, was intrigued with her first encounter with a Caucasian man. He was a big, burly six-foot five-inch American with wild red hair and beard. She stared at him intently, walking around and around him like he was a statue in the park. They had to drag her away from him and up to the hotel room. Later, when they noticed she was missing, they found her downstairs still staring at the red-bearded man. She was equally fascinated with her first sight of an African man. He, too, was tall, had very dark skin and wore his hair in a bushy Afro-style.

Whenever anyone was noticeably absent from the group they could usually be found riding the escalator up and down from floor to floor. At one point Sam mentioned that he had a hard time telling white people apart; they all looked alike to him. When Chet told him that is what white people say about the Chinese, he replied rather indignantly, "We all look very different. Can't they see that?"

As the years passed, they were all becoming more and more excited about the day when Chet would come to take them to America for a whole new way of life. Charlie was happy for them though he had opted not to make this big move. He thought it wonderful of Chet to do this for the family. His fulfillment in life came in finding Chet. That was enough for him.

Epilogue

At the beginning of November 1996, it finally came – the notice of approval from the government for their emigration to the U.S. The letter estimated the date of departure to be in February or March of 1997. This was to be the most exciting time of their lives. It was finally going to happen! Both families were so thrilled they could hardly believe it was just a couple of months away. Now they had to put all their plans into action. It was a little scary. It would be such a huge change for them – but very exciting.

The next few weeks, however, produced a devastating twist of fate. The trip to the U.S. would to be only for Gail and her family. Sam was seriously injured in what was first thought to be a motorcycle accident. Gail and John got him into a good hospital and paid for all his medical care, but his condition was critical. Gail telephoned Chet daily with reports on Sam's condition but could only report that it did not look good for his recovery. Sam was hospitalized for about three weeks in a coma, before succumbing. This was devastating for the family.

Later, as a more accurate account of his death came to

light and was better understood through clearer translation of the facts, they learned what had actually happened. Sam was working late one evening in late November. He was interviewing a family at their home on some police matter. After completing the interview, he rode off on his motorcycle. Witnesses said they saw him slow his motorcycle, stop, and turn off the engine, and immediately slumped over the bike and fell to the ground. He was rushed to the hospital and later diagnosed with an aneurism in the brain. He was known to have high blood pressure and this caused the wall of an artery or vein to rupture, interrupting the flow of blood to the brain. He was unconscious and became comatose. His lungs were not functioning properly, requiring him to be on a respirator. Gail and John brought in a specialist from Canton to take charge of his care. Sam never regained consciousness and died just before Christmas of 1996. His body was cremated and is buried near his parents.

His family had been very dependent on Sam and couldn't imagine how they would carry on without him. Chet had bought them a house in Toi Shan about a year earlier to make things a little easier and more convenient for them in their work. John, with his construction skills, had made sure the new house was in good shape. He spent weeks fixing it up and making any needed repairs to have it as nice as possible for them.

Losing Sam was extremely difficult for Charlene but, as the reality set in, she made the necessary adjustments and they began rebuilding their life without him. Charlene was a strong woman psychologically and realized that she had to take on the role of head of the family if they were to survive. She did all she could to make a stable home for the children and see that they finished their schooling and grew up strong. They would have to pull together and support each other. Wendy always slept with a picture of her dad in his police uniform next to her bed. Roy took his dad's death very hard but tried not show it outwardly.

They were living in the house in Toi Shan and not in the village at the time of Sam's death. They were puzzled and hurt by a seeming aloofness toward them from villagers - people they had known all their lives. It seemed to the family that many were simply avoiding them. None of the family understood if the relationship had been actually that superficial – good only as long as Sam was there to offer help – or if they feared being asked to asked to help or contribute money (which the family had no thought of doing), or that they just didn't know what to say or do. The children especially felt hurt by this treatment.

On top of all this sorrow and pain came the huge disappointment that Charlene and the children would not be allowed to come to the U.S. under Chet's sponsorship. Government regulations allowed them to enter the country ONLY if accompanied by a direct sibling of their sponsor. It was Sam who was Chet's sibling and since he had now passed away, the legal connection was lost. This was a sad time for all the family, especially after all those years of anticipation and preparation. They had lost the anchor of their life as a family and now would also lose their hope of a new future in America.

Gail and John were terribly shocked by Sam's death. Gail always went to him for advice and for his opinion on most everything. He would always listen and consider her queries and give her advice on the best thing to do. John felt very close to Sam also, and the families did many things together. In this extreme emergency, Gail and John bore the financial responsibilities for Sam's care and other family needs until other resources could be brought in to help.

Chet could scarcely believe what had happened. For him, having just met and truly loved a brother that he had not even known about for most of his life, who was coming to start a new life with him in the U. S., this was a deep loss. The regulations that prevented Sam's family from coming to this country angered him greatly. He felt that it had already been approved for them to come and now that was coldly rescinded at a time of great need. The joy of having Gail and her family here would fill much of that void, but it would take some time to accept the loss of Sam and the added disappointment of being unable to help care for his family as had been his dream.

Through some tough years of adjustment Charlene and the children stabilized their lives in Toi Shan. The children finished their schooling and Roy took a position in the police force at the same station where his dad had worked. He is married to a girl named Sally (for the benefit of the American side of the family's inability to remember Chinese names) who had a business as a florist and they now have a daughter named Lorraine.

Wendy graduated and went to New Zealand to go to college. She learned to speak English very well. She has since married a man named Ricky, who is a computer technician, and they have two children: a son, Roland, and a brand new baby girl, Regina. Charlene visited them recently when Regina was born and is contemplating moving to New Zealand to live.

The final emigration approval letter for Gail and John arrived in late January of 1997, about a month after Sam's death. It gave them a date in early March of 1997 for their departure to the U.S. It was going to be very hard for Gail and John to leave Charlene and the children, but this would be their only opportunity to come to America unless they wanted to go through the whole process again, waiting another seven or more years. If they were going to go, it had to be now.

Chet and Mavis paid for their airline tickets to the U.S. and scheduled the trip so they could spend a few days in Hong Kong visiting Susan, Charlie's daughter, before they left. Anxiety was at a peak level since none of them had ever flown anywhere before or, for that matter, even been inside an airplane. Their itinerary took them to Seoul, South Korea and, after a few hours layover, on to LAX where Chet would pick them up. Fortunately, the flight attendants on the plane to Seoul were Chinese and could advise them and help them understand where to go and how to get what they needed. They arrived in the U.S. on March 7, 1997. When they had cleared customs at LAX and Chet saw them coming up the ramp, it was like a big battle and burden had finally lifted from his shoulders. It was a time of unbounded excitement, anticipation, and joy for all.

Chet knew it would require a lot of space to accommodate four people and all their belongings. He had arranged to pick them up with a friend who drove a van so everyone and everything could be successfully tucked in.

The first few days were spent mostly adjusting to tall buildings, crowded highways, the difficulty of getting to other places with so little public transportation available, and general amazement at such a new way of life. Going to Santa Monica beach was the one thing they loved most. It was more like what they were used to in Toi Shan. They also loved going to places like the Angeles National Forest and the San Diego Zoo. They were used to being able to walk everywhere they wanted to go and liked a freedom of movement and open spaces.

Chet's translator friends spent time with all of them to help them communicate more effectively. The frustration of trying to speak to each other and other people about this totally new way of life, to be able to ask questions and understand the answers was a critical point for all of them. Having the help of the translators relieved much of the anxiety and tension.

Following the initial introduction to the American way of life, it was time for English-as-a-Second-Language (ESL) classes, getting a car, driving lessons, and drivers licenses.

They also joined a Southern Baptist Church that had a large Chinese community which would help them get to know other Chinese and ease into life in America. This, however, brought some serious culture clashes concerning the way they honored their ancestors along with other practices and beliefs that were very important to them. They were told by the church that if they were to be members they must get rid of all such symbols and practices because these things violated God's Commandments.

Food was another source of difficulty. John was adamant about wanting rice with every meal and having the food heavily salted. It was difficult to convince him of the connection between heavy use of salt and high blood pressure even though that could have been a significant factor in Sam's death. They always shopped at Chinese grocery stores in an effort to help the transition. Finally, Chet and Mavis prepared the food as they normally would and served it as they always did so their newly-arrived family members would get used to eating that way. It took some time for John to accept the American ways of preparing food.

Several months had now gone by. John was used to being very busy and active in the business of construction but the hope of finding a job was becoming more problematical. He was not thrilled with the ESL classes and was not making enough progress in speaking English well enough to apply for jobs and meet the many requirements other than his abilities and the quality of his work. John was in touch with a cousin of his who lived in Brooklyn, New York, and worked in construction. He offered to help John learn the ins and outs of the American construction business and establish himself for work. This was a wonderful opportunity for John, so he flew to New York to work with his cousin.

Gail flew back to New York several times to visit him and in October of 1997 went there to stay. She had an opportunity to work at a laundromat. It helped them become better established financially and independently. Since the girls were enrolled in college here, they stayed with Chet and Mavis to finish their classes for the semester. At the beginning of the year they, too, moved to New York. It was important to keep the family together and too difficult and expensive to keep flying back and forth. Misty and Melody both completed college in New York state and Misty is continuing her studies for an MBA. Both girls are now married and living happy lives in the New York area. Chet and Mavis flew there to attend and be a part of their graduations and weddings. As their careers and family continue to develop and grow the New Yorkers do have thoughts of returning to the west coast where it all began. It is where their long broken family circle first became reconnected and whole again and where they began their new life in America.

Acknowledgements

Writing this book was somewhat of an identity search for the author also. I had not attempted a biography before and did not know if I could accomplish it. My long-time friend, Patricia Dunlap, became acquainted with Chet Lee when they worked for the same company. Pat told me about his life and said, "Someone should write this story!" followed by, "Why don't you?" From a copy of facts about his life written by a friend, Karen Murphy, it was obvious that this was an intriguing story. After meeting Chet the e-mails began flying back and forth between us in my pursuit of presenting these fascinating facts in story form.

Chet and his wife, Mavis, provided a tremendous amount of documentation, photos, insights, and won-tons. (I know why they are called won-tons – they are <u>won</u>-derful and I could eat <u>tons</u> of them!) Chet read all the sections as they were completed to validate details of the story in process.

A huge thanks is owed to all those who translated the Chinese letters and documents into English especially Chang-Huey Wu, Duncan Wu, and John Wang, as well as Scarlett Hu, Ken Ho, and Jill Hu. The depth of information from Chet's family, Charlie, Sam, Gail and their families was immeasurable.

My children were a wonderful cheering section for me. I am also eternally grateful for the encouragement, support, and downright *nagging* to start writing from Mary Rose Betten and Tricia Bevan over the years. Tricia did the final editing of the book to catch any of my bashings of the rules of grammar. Nan Hunt provided the idea for the title and Peter Kraus gave advice on the cover design.

Both Chet and I would be very interested in responses from readers through web pages with Outskirts Press and/or www.ApawnofFate.com

.

Printed in the United States
134058LV00001BA/224/P